Maid in Taiwan

BARBARA NORTH

OMF BOOKS

Copyright © Overseas Missionary Fellowship
(formerly China Inland Mission)

First published 1984

ISBN 9971-83-773-0

OMF BOOKS are distributed by
OMF, 404 South Church Street,
Robesonia, Pa. 19551, USA
and
OMF, Belmont, The Vine,
Sevenoaks, Kent, TN13 3TZ, UK
and other OMF offices.

Published by Overseas Missionary Fellowship (IHQ) Ltd,
2 Cluny Road, Singapore 1025, Republic of Singapore.
Printed by Richard Clay (S.E. Asia) Pte Ltd.

Contents

1 *A Textile Mill in Bradford*

Stepping out of those swinging hospital doors, a peaky, white-faced little five year old, I rushed into my father's arms. Never would I let him go again! The six weeks of scarlet fever had seemed like eternity.

It was a cold, foggy, November afternoon as we clambered into my father's old Austin Seven. As we travelled home in the little box-shaped car which seemed to dance from one side of the road to the other, we could just about see the grey dry-stone walling on either side of the narrow road. Daddy had to open the window to see where we were going at one point, and we could hear the strange sound of sheep coughing in the fog. As we went downhill, down into the centre of Bradford, visibility was worsening all the time.

Daddy was telling me about a new 'auntie' who had come to live in our home and look after me while he was out piano-tuning. Neither of the two previous housekeepers had stayed more than a month, so it was with some misgivings that he had put yet another advert in the local paper. But this one looked as if she might stay: an older woman who seemed concerned and kindly and had worked in a mill all her life. Now that her blind mother had died she was looking for a job.

'What's her name?' I asked.

'Miss Robinson ... Auntie Sarah.'

My parents had separated when I was two and my father had brought me to the north of England, wanting to get back to his roots now that the second world war had started. Living with relatives had not been a success. But my father's tuning connections built up when piano-playing suddenly became popular, so he was able to buy his own house and be independent.

Now the car was crawling in low gear up Wibsey Bank on the other side of Bradford. It was nearly dark and the blackouts were being pulled down at people's windows as lights were switched on. Car headlights had to be dipped. All the smoke from mill chimneys and fires, as well as petrol fumes, was turning the fog into a real pea-souper. There would be chaos in the next hour or so when the hooters went and all the mills 'loosed' with the factory workers pouring out.

We were up to the roundabout. Just a few yards further on we pulled up outside a large grey-stone terraced house. My dad carried me into the warm back kitchen where a plump, smiling, grey-haired woman was buttering bread for tea.

'So you'll be Barbara,' she said, and gave me a big hug, just like a granny would. I didn't have a granny or a mother so I took to this warm, loving 'auntie' immediately.

2

'Now then, love, you'll be right hungry after all those weeks in hospital, so sit yourself down and tuck into those corned beef sandwiches.'

This wartime special treat was followed by pink blancmange and red jelly.

Auntie Sarah stayed with us for five years, through air-raid sirens, rationing and the rest. I loved to hear stories of her life in the mill, especially when she was young ...

** ** ** **

'Sarah, Sarah! It's nearly ten past six! You'll be late if you don't look sharp. I'm not waiting for you.'

'All right, I'm getting up,' Sarah yelled back to her sister. She threw the bedclothes back, stretched, got out and reached for her clothes. Five minutes later she had run down the forty steps from the attic to the cellar-kitchen and was having a quick wash by the sink. The cold water stung her cheeks and gave her a clean, fresh feeling. But she would have given all she possessed to have been able to go back to bed and have her sleep out.

Nellie and Sarah worked at the same mill and could make it in nine minutes. Nellie never liked hurrying but Sarah held on to her bed till the last possible moment! Now she glanced at the clock as she gulped her tea and bolted a slice of bread and jam down — it was twenty past six. She ran through the passage that led to the front of the back-to-back houses where they lived, and down to the end of the street, her clogs clattering along the flagstones. She walked quickly up the hill against the wind that

3

whipped the brown shawl around her thin face.
Down a back-alley and she was there.

She arrived at the mill just as the 'Penny-Hoil'
man (the gateman who took a penny off your wages
if you were late) was closing the gate. He smiled and
said, 'You've nobbut just made it.'

Sarah grinned and hurried on. She still had six
flights of steps to climb to get to Number Three. The
thought of the overlooker and his alley-strap spurred
her on. She arrived a bit breathless, just as the engine
went on and the wheels began to turn. The warm
stuffy air filled with particles of wool met you as you
entered. Sarah rolled up her coat and put it in the
locker at the bottom of the 'gate'.

The room had an aisle down the centre, with the
spinning frames on either side. There were great big
wheels and belts overhead connecting the machines
with pulleys. The spinning machine took the good
Botany wool that Bradford was famous for and spun
it to thick cotton.

Sarah saw George the overlooker coming out of
his gate at the far end of the room. She turned on her
machine slowly to avoid breaking any ends. Meanwhile George passed by, swishing the alley-strap and
cracking it on the floor, which sent all the fluff flying
under the frames and gave the room a swept-up
appearance. Sarah was glad to be well down the
gate and out of reach of it. She was busy watching
her ends and mending any that broke. She was a
spinner now and minded three sides, a frame and a
half. When the bobbins of thick wool were full she
would stop the machine and shout 'Doff here' —

4

then three or four twelve-year-old 'doffers' would appear to take the full bobbins off and replace them with empty ones. Then the machine was set on again. The noise was deafening but most spinners became so accustomed to it that after a while they didn't notice it. There was no chance to talk, because they couldn't leave their sides, though occasionally they would call over to somebody nearby. They often sang as they worked. Sarah was sadly out of tune but as nobody could hear her it didn't matter.

The girls had just finished doffing the machine at eight o'clock when one of the shop-floor lads walked down the aisle with a tray, shouting 'Tea up'. Everyone fetched their pint pots containing tea and sugar, and the boy took them to fill with hot water. When he got back the great wheels were slowing down and stopping for the half-hour break. The spinners turned their machines off and everyone went to their buffets by the window, took their sandwiches out and started to eat breakfast.

Sarah drew up her buffet near Annie Shaw, who was on the next machine. They talked about where they had been at the weekend, about boys they knew and what was going on at the chapel. Sarah often went with Annie to Eastbrook Hall on Sunday evenings and then to the Open Air meeting on the Wool Exchange steps in Market Street, when young people walked up and down to get to know each other. At that time there was no means of meeting the opposite sex except at chapel or work — there were no youth clubs or dance halls — so the crowd which turned out on Market Street was often so great that the police found it hard work to keep them moving.

Just a month ago the great evangelist Gipsy Smith had come to hold meetings at Eastbrook Hall. For some time Sarah had admired Annie's stand as a Christian, and noticed her thoughtfulness for others, her unconscious joy and her practical commonsense. She hadn't been able to put .her finger on what it was that made her different from the rest, but she knew instinctively it had something to do with her relationship with God. Sarah wanted to know this inner strength herself, so when Annie took her along to hear the evangelist her heart was already prepared. She knew only too well how she needed forgiveness and cleansing from Jesus who had died for her. So she responded to the invitation to go out with others to acknowledge Him to be her Saviour and Lord.

I didn't appreciate all this as a child, of course. But one of my clearest memories is of her sitting in the kitchen rocking-chair with her eyes closed.

'Are you sleeping, Auntie?' I'd whisper. 'No, I'm talking to Jesus. Just leave me alone a minute,' she'd reply.

Moments like this left a profound impression on me.

It was not till years later that she told me how, from that very first day of my arrival from hospital, she had begun to pray daily that my father and I would one day come to know Jesus as our Saviour, as she had. She had spent the whole of her working life in that mill, as Christ's ambassador, until at the age of sixty she asked the Lord for new guidance and He led her to us. Eventually she left us to look after an ailing sister for whom she felt responsible, and after that we did not employ any more housekeepers. No one could replace her in our hearts.

Father's health seemed to be failing so we moved to the seaside. He was restless and we went out a lot — I enjoyed going to the cinema with him twice a week, though I felt rather sick when we went to the all-in-wrestling! We went to all the seaside shows too and, fascinated by the theatre, I was determined to be an actress. I even persuaded my father to pay for private drama lessons. Dad had his dreams too, of emigrating to Rhodesia to the sun, but he settled in the end for the South Coast and so we were on the move again.

We found Peacehaven on a hot June day. There was a bungalow for sale, way back on the gorse-covered Downs with a superb view of the English Channel. What's more, there was a plot of land attached, just right for a pony. But on wet wintry days my twenty-minute walk on a lonely unmade road, followed by two buses and a train to get to school, made my father wonder if he had done the right thing. But God was able to incorporate what was perhaps an unwise decision into His plan.

Now that my father's rheumatoid arthritis had crippled his hands he was no longer able to work. A pony was out of the question and I had to be content to wander around in jodhpurs. To make things worse, I could not settle at my new school. My Yorkshire accent was ridiculed and for once in my life I felt rejected by my class-mates. I was just thirteen. During these traumatic days I found my escape in reading. The school library was a treasure house to be explored. I was particularly gripped by a series of biographies of famous Christian pioneers, and one in particular with whom I could identify was Mary Slessor, who used to read her Bible propped against her loom in a Scottish woollen mill. She was timid and afraid even of crossing the street, yet bravely set out in God's strength to Central Africa, to paddle on crocodile-infested rivers in order to share the Gospel of Christ with those who had never heard.

My father discovered a small but lively Girls' Club attached to the tiny asbestos-built church on the coast road in Peacehaven, and encouraged me to join. The leader had a personal relationship with Jesus Christ, as Auntie had. I watched her carefully. By this time I knew that to become a Christian was all or nothing. No half measures would do — I had seen enough superficiality in my young life already. My mind was full of questions — was the Bible true and reliable? What about the suffering of innocent people? Week after week all the old chestnuts and more were put to my long-suffering leader. Over cups of tea and cakes in their tiny bungalow, she and her friend tried to help me understand the Bible. They both knew the Scriptures well and their prayers joined Auntie's that my father and I would soon find the Lord. But by now I was popular again at school, excelling in games and drama, and had no desire to be an 'odd man out' again. Strangely

8

enough, I had announced to my friends that I wanted to become a missionary, but it seemed that as yet I hadn't even the courage to become a Christian! I was looking for an adventurous life and was determined not to be disappointed.

My happiness was short-lived, however. In a desperate attempt to fight the ill-health that dogged Father, we took to caravan-life and moved again and again. Those lean, unsettled days involved adjustments to another two schools. Our Peacehaven friends tried to link us with churches, but I had taken to cycling with a friend on Sundays. We ended up in a ground-floor flat in Brighton. Then out of the blue someone from the basement knocked on the door one evening.

'Would you like to join us on a coach-party going to Harringay to hear Billy Graham?'

Why not! Although I had not been in touch with Christians for two years, the question-mark was still there. I was staggered by the vast number of people in the stadium and stirred by the singing. It seemed that Billy Graham was speaking to me alone as he stressed how some of us had known God's call on our lives for many years and yet, because of our pride, our questions and our fears, we were continually putting off the moment of commitment to Him. He warned that as we went on hardening our hearts against Him, His voice would become softer until we might no longer be able to hear Him.

By 'getting up out of my seat' at Harringay I was beginning to realize that the Holy Spirit of God had put His hand upon me from my earliest days, using the sweet influence of Auntie and others to woo me to Himself. I knew I could not afford to wait any longer in seeking His forgiveness, and so I put my hand in His to start the greatest adventure of all — following His leading and direction for the rest of my life.

I was put in touch with a 'keen' church, but I was afraid of the Youth Fellowship! Everyone seemed so confident, knowing where to turn in their Bibles, talking in clichés I could not understand. I was smothered with welcome, but doubted if anyone really cared if I turned up again or not. Actually, they came to find me when I did not appear the following Sunday. But a stubborn streak stopped me from going again.

What was I looking for as I tried each church in turn on Sunday evenings? I was afraid to get involved, determined to stay on the fringe until I found the perfect church. One thing was for sure — I was spiritually hungry, for the Lord had planted a desire to be fed in this new-born Christian. But my wandering around like a spiritual gipsy was preventing me from being built up into the Church, the Body of Christ.

It was not long before boyfriends, dances and rebellion over parental authority all took the edge off my desire to walk with the Lord. I was ready to drop out of school and really live it up! But at this point my father began to get seriously worried. He hadn't wanted me to go overboard as a religious fanatic, but perhaps this was worse! Quite suddenly, he came to a decision and announced: 'We must go back to Peacehaven.' I was dumbfounded, angry and frustrated. Peacehaven was far too cut off from the Brighton scene. My over-protective father knew this only too well, and went on to say, 'What's more, I think I shall start going to that little church on the coast-road. I think it would do you good to go back there too!'

I could not believe my ears. Father had always felt God had given him a bad deal in his life, and had no time for churches. What a change of attitude! The Holy Spirit was working in strange and wonderful ways.

So we moved back to Peacehaven, and I didn't leave school after all. My father began going to church, not missing a Sunday, and it was not long before the pastor led him to a personal trust in Christ as his Saviour. The church family took him lovingly into their fellowship and this brought much inner healing. I too became involved and began to grow as a Christian. Before long I was given a Sunday School class to teach and to my amazement discovered how enjoyable it was.

Now that I was asking God to show me His plan for the future, the thought of missionary work overseas still had its magical appeal. But when I asked people what training was needed, they all seemed rather vague. Nurses and teachers featured largely in missionary magazines; I knew I would never be a nurse, but teaching appealed. However, with my chequered school career it seemed impossible that I would be accepted at any college. When I found myself welcomed at a good college further along the coast, I recognized the Lord's hand yet again.

Suddenly my father's health deteriorated quickly and a few weeks later he died, having found peace with God in a windswept cliff-top community aptly called Peacehaven.

I grieved for a long time. As college days ended I realized I wanted to go back to the industrial North. Teaching in Bradford was totally absorbing at first; then as I got into the swing of it I became more involved in the outreach of a Mission Church in the centre of the city. It was surrounded by mills and warehouses, with Asians moving in all around. There was an overseas mission field on our doorstep.

Feeling my need for further Bible training, I enrolled at the Bible Training Institute in Glasgow, but my time there was brought abruptly to an end as I was summoned to care for a needy uncle and aunt. When that responsibility ended, my cousin startled me by asking, 'Now that you've had the extra training, have you thought of Scripture teaching in a secondary school?'

The downtown secondary school in Halifax, home of carpet and biscuit factories, was a far cry from the trusting six-year-olds of my previous school. I doubted whether I would survive a month! The tall leather-jacketed youths frightened me and the seemingly mature, sophisticated girls unnerved me. How could I make the Bible and the Christian life relevant to these down-to-earth, no-nonsense young people? It was a tremendous challenge and one which I needed every scrap of wisdom from above to accept. I realized that if ever I was to get through, I needed to be with them on the games field and on school outings, to have fun and relax with them. I needed to have access to plenty of good audio-visual aids in the classroom. They needed to meet 'invited' Christians from other walks of life willing to try and answer their questions and doubts, and to be involved in projects that showed Christianity in action. An understanding Headmaster and staff backed me up and I discovered the joy and responsibility of being able to relax with a class, sitting on the top of a desk discussing the issues of life and death.

**   **   **   **

'Can you think of a good reason for not going to South East Asia? What are you waiting for — a special feeling?' This was the challenge I had to face at the Overseas Missionary Fellowship conference in Derbyshire. Several friends from Bible College had joined the OMF and I regularly met with a prayer group focusing on East Asia. However, I had imagined that the possibility of going overseas now was pretty slim. I had found my niche teaching in a pagan school in England. Why go overseas?

Yet I no longer had any responsibilities in England; I was free. I was fit. I had always wanted to be a missionary overseas and I was still not too old. There was no reason why anyone in Britain could not hear the Gospel, but in many other parts of the world there were few Christians to share the

Good News among so many. Was there a place for me in South East Asia — perhaps among the tribal people of the Philippines or the students of Indonesia? Yet I did not think I could cope with the loneliness of village life, or be intellectual enough for the student world.

It was on a sunny morning in the lounge of the lovely old building at Swanwick, during that conference, that I was first introduced to the island of Taiwan, or Formosa as it was then called. Gordon and Margaret Aldis had been there for many years, involved particularly with the Chinese student population and seeing a great hunger for the Gospel. But Margaret began to speak about the great changes coming on that small island as industrial zones replaced farmland and hundreds of young people were sweeping into the cities, living in poor accommodation in and around the factory areas. Many were disorientated and lonely. Their families needed the money, but apart from the long hours standing by the machines they had nowhere to go. No one seemed to care for them as individuals. There were few Christians. Would we pray for the Taiwanese Church as they sought ways to share the love of Christ with these needy young people ... 'Are any of you willing to go and help alongside?' was Margaret's final remark.

This was it! I felt I could see myself in that setting. Industrial areas, pollution, secondary-modern-type Chinese teenagers and factories like the one where Auntie had come to know Christ. Didn't someone say that a call was the trend of a

14

lifetime? My whole being responded. 'Lord, here am I, send me.'

My enthusiastic offer to the missionary society did not receive the most encouraging response from the Candidates' Secretary! I was told to go away and pray about it. Perhaps later if I still felt God's call to South East Asia, I could write to them.

As it happened, I was due to go on holiday with a friend to Brighton immediately after the conference. So I walked on the beach where, a hundred years before, Hudson Taylor had contemplated China's millions who had never had the opportunity of hearing the Gospel. There he had made his covenant with God and the China Inland Mission, predecessor of the OMF, was born.

Doubts and questions came to my mind. How would I cope with the Chinese language? I certainly hadn't a natural flair for languages — I had had to be coached through my GCE French. What about Chinese food? I had been brought up on vegetarian health foods to please my father. As these doubts arose, the assurance that I should go forward was unmistakable and the verse from the Bible that came to me then, and has stuck with me during fourteen years in Taiwan, was, 'My grace is sufficient for you, for My strength is made perfect in weakness.' So, after numerous letters, interviews, forms to fill in, doctors' and psychologists' reports, I was finally accepted as a candidate for the Overseas Missionary Fellowship. Designation — Taiwan.

It was hard leaving Ostler School in Halifax.

'Oh miss, you'll come back with slit-eyes.'

'You'll marry a Chinese, miss.'

'Will you send us pictures and stamps?'

I have warm memories of a school I had threatened to leave a dozen times, but which had proved to be the best training ground one could ever have for reaching factory young people in Taiwan.

Renewed links with the asbestos (now brick-built) church in Peacehaven and the congregation's strong desire to stand with me in support and prayer were the most positive encouragements I could receive. How I needed their prayers in the years ahead! Auntie too, now aged 84 but still bright, was just thrilled that I was going overseas to share the Gospel with factory workers like herself. The wheel had turned full circle.

2   *Export to Taiwan*

'Good-bye, Big Sister.'

'*Zai-jian*, till we meet again.'

The Chen family clustered around on the platform as I leaned out of the carriage window. Mrs Chen, elegant as always, was wearing a tight-fitting *cheongsam* of green silk with a Mandarin collar. Seventeen-year-old Jye, dressed casually in a sports shirt, had an infectious grin. He was teasing me about the amount of luggage I was taking. His fifteen-year-old brother was wearing his light-khaki school uniform. With a crew cut and peaked cap, he looked like a student from an American military academy. Bespectacled, thoughtful, he was solemnly presenting me with a map of the route I was taking. Eleven-year-old Siau-Mei gave me a hug. We had been to so many places together, and I had taught her to swim. Her Chinese was clear and simple, a joy to listen to.

I had lived with the Chen family for nearly two years. Could it really be so long since we had docked in Keelung in North Taiwan, having just spent two months in Singapore for orientation? The *Anping* had brought us over the choppy Taiwan Straits to this island, about a hundred miles off the south-east coast of China. It was so near the mainland, so Chinese in its way of life. But it had a Nationalist government, diametrically opposed to the Communist régime, and therefore there was no communication between the two Chinas.

I had travelled with Moira, another new missionary whose home was in the north of Scotland, and together we had been introduced into this Christian Chinese home only a few days after our arrival. Mr Chen had died suddenly, leaving the family in a state of deep shock, and their pastor had suggested that to take in two western girls would provide an added source of income. It would also be an excellent way for the children to improve their English.

So we moved into their wooden, Japanese-style, middle-class home in Taipei. There were lots of misunderstandings but also lots of fun. We had a tussle of wills over how much English or Chinese was spoken, and found the family often won! Nevertheless it was a relief to talk in English for a while after a hard day in Language School.

It was in their home one day that we experienced our first major earth-tremor. The rest of the family were out when we heard what sounded like heavy lorries rumbling past. Then the whole house began to shake. Moira automatically ran to grab the large clock swaying on the wall, while I helplessly held on to the refrigerator as the floor shook beneath us. Suddenly it all stopped. But our legs felt like jelly for hours afterwards.

Living with the Chens brought an air of normality into those first two years of gruelling language study. Family life with its joys and quarrels is very similar whatever culture you move into: there were times when we did not belong, but Moira and I had the comfort of being isolated together. At other times we felt secure within the warmth of the family circle, watching TV and eating meals together. Mrs Chen was an excellent cook and we became quite adventurous in trying all kinds of Chinese food. The family, on the other hand, were more cautious in sampling our western-style dishes! We came to realize how close the family bonds are in the Chinese way of life. We marvelled at the number of relatives the Chens were in touch with, and the close interaction there seemed to be, whether it was in borrowing or lending money or in just being generally helpful. What a privilege it had been to live with a Chinese family, and how I was going to miss them all!

The long, crowded express train slowly pulled out of Taipei station heading for South Taiwan. As I sat back on my green plastic seat next to the window, I was grateful to see the compartment ceiling fans begin to whirr and rotate from side to side as the train picked up speed. The breeze was welcome against my hot sticky skin in that stuffy, humid compartment.

A formal announcement was made in Chinese welcoming us aboard. I found that I understood the gist of it, and was pleased. I was beginning to gain confidence now in my knowledge of Chinese, but had

19

not found language study easy. Five hours a day in Language School, and four more hours shut up in our rooms listening to tape recordings and writing out our homework! From being a confident, articulate teacher in England I had been reduced to feeling like a small child in kindergarten, and had gone through the most awful identity crisis. Much of the time I had felt frustrated, helpless and useless. Even my good relationship with Moira had been threatened by deep feelings of jealousy when the Chens and others compared our progress. But there had been hilarious moments too when we realized what howlers we were making just by using the wrong tone. Never had I needed a sense of humour so much. Never did I want to let off steam so much as after a hard day, trying to write and remember the Chinese character script. I would go home, close my door, put on a pop record and really let go and dance. That was one of my particular escape mechanisms and I was thankful for it. But my anchor was the fact that I knew God had called me to this land, so I believed that one day I would really be able to communicate. My greatest encouragement was the knowledge that friends at Peacehaven and elsewhere were praying specifically for this.

I looked out of the train window. We were still in the suburbs and the ribbon development would continue for a long time to come. We passed grey concrete buildings, terraced blocks of houses and shops. Grey wooden slatted houses were being pulled down with new high-rise buildings supported by bamboo scaffolding taking their place.

Narrow streets were filled with buses, cars and people.

We passed a level-crossing which looked like the starting line of some great race. Motor-bikes were impatiently revving up, anxious for the train to pass and to be first off the mark. One rider had a basket of chickens behind him, another had panes of glass stacked precariously high. The driver of a truck filled with squealing pigs sat on his horn, irritably edging in between a red taxi with people leaning out of its windows and a motor-scooter. A mother in a large sun hat was astride the scooter, balancing it with both feet on the ground. One small child was standing on the platform in front of her, and two others were clinging on behind. On the far side of the crossing was a wheeled restaurant, a movable stall with stools upturned on the top and a bottled-gas cylinder strapped at the back. There were people everywhere!

I had become accustomed to crowds. Taiwan is a small island only as big as Wales. Much of it is mountainous, so the majority of its seventeen million people are squashed into this western coastal plain. It is extremely fertile, but cities and industry are mushrooming and in many areas taking over the rich farmland.

The train compartment was crowded too. Some people were standing, others sitting on the arms of seats. Children were either asleep, eating or making a terrible din. Next to me sat a smartly-dressed young man reading a newspaper. I could only recognize two characters from the headlines — I was still out of my depth when it came to reading newspaper Chinese.

A smart young lady attendant was threading her way through the long compartment with a tray of tea-bags, from which we were invited to select the blend of our choice. I chose jasmine and emptied the bag into a glass balanced in a metal holder against the window. The gentleman next to me leaned over and emptied his small packet of green tea into the other glass. A little later a young fellow would come swaying along with an enormous kettle and deftly pour hot water into each glass. He would appear twice more on our seven-hour journey to replenish our glasses.

It was at this point that my neighbour turned to me and asked in clear, precise English, 'Where are you going?'

'To Kaohsiung,' I replied and smiled. I felt a surge of excitement at the thought of leaving Taipei and those tedious hours at Language School far behind. At long last I was going to be in touch with some of the people God had called me to meet — the factory workers of Taiwan.

Kaohsiung is a large port in the south west of the island, two hundred miles from the capital, Taipei. It is also a large industrial city. At that time, Taiwan's first large export processing zone was almost completed and another about to begin there. Heavy industry was booming, with steel yards, ironworks and shipyards.

My neighbour seemed delighted that I was

going to live in Kaohsiung, and I discovered that he was a department-head in one of the largest electronic factories in the zone. Coincidence? No! Just another of God's delightful ways of linking people together.

'How long have you been in Taiwan?' he asked with interest.

'Nearly two years,' I replied.

'Can you speak Chinese?'

'A little,' I grinned.

Perhaps I should try out my Chinese on him now. But no, he was much too keen to improve his English.

Then came the golden question. The one I was asked about five times a day, each time giving me an opportunity to speak of my Heavenly Father.

'Why have you come here?' my companion enquired.

'To share the good news about Jesus Christ,' I replied.

He looked puzzled. Now I just had to speak in Chinese. I fumblingly told him how I had come to know God in a personal way through Jesus, and how I believed God had called me to Taiwan to stand alongside Chinese Christians. We wanted to tell those who have never heard about God's love for the whole world and His desire that all should trust in Him.

My new friend was quiet and thoughtful. I wasn't sure how much of my Chinese he had understood. His only reply was to comment politely, 'You speak Chinese very well'.

I knew that my tones had gone haywire and my vocabulary was still very limited. I did not want a false compliment, but I tried to accept it as kindly encouragement. I was jolted by his next question, though.

'Do you get a good salary?' He sounded concerned.

'Enough for my daily needs,' I evaded.

I toyed with the idea of going into detail about praying to God for our financial needs and seeing Him answer in remarkable ways. It was true that Moira and I had lived on a shoestring in those early days in Taipei. We had had many unexpected expenses, especially when the weather became unpleasantly wet and cold during the winter months, for we had not anticipated the need to bring warm clothing. Sometimes we had no money between us, even running out of our Mission allocation. But when some real need arose, like a trip to the dentist, the money always came, sometimes from home, sometimes from Chinese friends. It was always enough. We never had to borrow. We thrilled at the privilege of being in a position of utter dependence on the Lord and proving His faithfulness in this way.

Before I could assemble my thoughts to explain any further, my friend asked, 'What do you think of Taiwan?'

'Oh! It's a beautiful country and the people here are so friendly to strangers like myself.' I answered him enthusiastically, and I was not just being polite.

He smiled and we both looked out of the window. We had left the city sprawl by now and were out in the open country, looking on to green rice paddies. Labourers in coolie hats were walking along the sides of the irrigation ditches between the fields. The bamboo poles slung over their shoulders had pails balanced at each end filled with water, which they were carefully tipping on to the young shoots on either side. A man was leading a water buffalo along an unmade road. In the distance the mountains, range upon range, rose majestically in weird and wonderful shapes like those on the Chinese paintings I had seen in museums.

'This is my home country,' commented my friend. 'Most of the people living in this area are Hakka Chinese like me. Our ancestors came over from the mainland in the seventeenth century, about the same time that the ancestors of the Taiwanese came. But they were from further south in China, and we've remained distinct to this day. They make up more than three-quarters of the population, but we Hakka are only about 15 percent. We speak a different Chinese dialect, as I'm sure you know, and we tend to be more conservative, and probably more economical too. We would tend to build our villages on the sides of the hills where you can't grow things, rather than waste good farmland as the Taiwanese do!'

The coastal plain was narrowing and the mountains suddenly seemed much nearer. Their slopes were covered with small bushes.

'This area is famous for tea-plantations,' my companion remarked. 'We shall be at my home town of Miaoli soon.'

We passed several temples before the train slowed to a halt. All were very similar, built in the very ornate Chinese traditional style, in blue and pink tiles. In the countryside we had passed numerous mini-temples and wayside shrines. I was not surprised, as I had heard that Taiwan has more temples per head of population than any other country in South East Asia. The religion of Taiwan is confusing to analyse, being a mixture of Animism, Buddhism and Taoism.

'Are you a Buddhist?' I asked my friend.

'I don't have much time for religion,' he replied. 'But if I did not worship the ancestors my parents would be very angry.'

I was going to question him further, but we had drawn into Miaoli station.

It was pandemonium. A lot of country people were getting off with their bundles, and the platform was crowded with others eager to get on. Outside the window, vendors were calling out their wares, weighed down with trays of lunch-packs, packets of dried meat, glacé fruits, hard-boiled eggs stewed in tea and canned drinks. Military police were striding up and down the platform telling· people to wait till everyone got off before boarding the train. A consignment of young soldiers squatted at the far end of the station, probably waiting for another train. National Service is compulsory in Taiwan.

A minor dispute was going on behind us, with two men each claiming the same seat. They sounded very excited and I couldn't understand their Mandarin very well. My friend told me that they were Mainlanders from one of the northern provinces in China, probably ex-soldiers who had come over with Chiang Kai-shek in 1951 when he fled to Taiwan from the mainland of China at the Communist take-over. Mainlanders and their families now make up ten percent of the population. My companion assured me that these two were not as angry as they sounded! They had discovered they both had the same compartment and seat number written on their tickets. One of them had gone off to find the ticket inspector who would no doubt find him another seat on the train.

We were now right in the mountains. The diesel train was chugging along slowly and we went through several tunnels, coming out on high embankments with quiet forested valleys stretching below us. It was very beautiful.

'Do you get homesick?' my friend asked.

'Sometimes,' I answered guardedly. I seemed to have a love-hate relationship with this beautiful island. One moment I revelled in the adventure and privilege of being here; the next I would be filled with nostalgia for my own country, for old friends, English meadows, long summer evenings, strong cold winds, baked beans.

In the early days I wrote lots of letters, needing to escape home when life in this strange culture seemed too hard to take. Every letter I received from my homeland boosted my lowered morale and deflated ego, for I needed to be assured that someone cared, and that someone was praying.

I was jerked back to Taiwan as we emerged from the last tunnel and began crossing long bridges over wide river-beds. The soldiers guarding the bridges looked tired and careworn. They were a visual reminder that Taiwan was militarily prepared to combat any Mainland aggression. Other soldiers were piling sand-bags in readiness for the typhoon season from May until October. At present streams trickled through the river beds and melons, asparagus and beans were growing there. I had been told that when typhoons sweep over the island, those almost dry river beds could, within hours, become wide, wild, raging rivers.

We stopped at a small town — I could not make out the characters that gave its name. A whole crowd of giggling girls boarded the train, dressed in mini-skirts and carrying pink suitcases. They were taller than most Chinese girls and had large brown eyes.

'They are tribal girls, aren't they?' I whispered. My companion nodded.

'They might be coming to Kaohsiung to work in the factories. You know that the aboriginal people were the first inhabitants to come to the island, don't you? They are from Malay stock, I think. When our ancestors came over from the

Mainland, the tribal people were driven into the mountains. They used to be greatly feared as head-hunters — do you know the story of Gau-Hong? His statue is at Wu-She, near here.'

'No, do tell me.' I was glad that he was feeling more talkative now he knew I could understand Chinese.

'Well, two hundred years ago there lived a tribe of head-hunters in the mountains back there. The Taiwanese were terrified of them and tried to think of ways to stop their raids. One of their number, a courageous man named Gau-Hong, decided to go and live in the mountains for a while, trying to befriend the tribal people and learn their language.

'He succeeded, and gained their trust, becoming their friend. He almost persuaded them to give up the cruel practice of head-hunting.

'But one day they came to explain to Gau-Hong that their largest festival of the year was about to take place. This time, however, instead of raiding the lowlands, they would take just one head. The gods had demanded this.

'Gau-Hong tried to persuade them to change their mind, but he failed. "Well then," he said at last, "if you must take one head tomorrow morning, kill the first traveller who comes along the hill track."

'Next morning, a man in a brown coat and a red hat came riding along the appointed path. The head-hunters sprang out and clubbed him to death. Only when he lay dead did they recognize their friend Gau-Hong. The year was 1769, and from that day head-hunting ceased in Taiwan.'

In the middle of the story, I remembered that I had heard it before. A Christian teacher in Language School had told it to us, drawing the parallel with the sacrifice that Jesus Christ made on the cross for us as our substitute, our representative.

I pointed out the analogy to my travelling companion and he looked most interested. But whatever he was going to say next got lost as the compartment's sliding door opened and two young attendants called out —

'*Byen-Dangs!* Lunch boxes!'

My friend insisted on buying me one. They were good value for money. The round tin boxes passed to us were hot, and contained a large portion of boiled rice with a good piece of pork, a few vegetables and gravy poured on the top. We unwrapped our disposable chopsticks and began to eat.

There was silence for a while. Then I smiled at my companion's next question. In Taiwan society it was not considered too personal, and I had been asked it a hundred times already since arriving.

'Why aren't you married?'

'I haven't met the right person yet,' I countered. It sounded a bit glib and he grinned.

'Don't be too choosy,' he warned. He was probably thinking it very strange that my family and friends at home had not introduced me to

30

someone suitable by now.

In Taiwan, although young people usually marry later than their western counterparts, it is almost unheard of to remain single after a certain age. I was later to discover that I could identify with Chinese Christian girls who were trying to hold out under family pressure to marry a Buddhist, and wait for a Christian partner. I was to see some remarkable answers to prayer on this account, as well as some amusing situations when well-meaning Chinese friends tried to do something for me!

As we travelled further south, I became more hot and sticky and had the beginnings of a headache. My companion smoothed Tiger Balm oil on his forehead. He passed the small tin to me and I tried a little. In spite of its strong, almost overpowering smell it was immediately cooling and seemed to revive me.

The vegetation was changing and here in the south the rice crop was being harvested. They were able to plant three crops a year, as opposed to two in the north. Taiwan produces enough rice for its own consumption, and is even able to export some overseas. We were passing banana plantations too, and I noticed that many of the clusters were covered with plastic bags to prevent them from ripening too soon. Then there were fields of sugar cane and pineapples. We passed a few Taiwanese farms, whose doors all seemed to face south. Barking dogs, chickens and ducks ran free in the yards, and a bamboo grove surrounded most of the farms, protecting them from strong winds or bright sunshine.

I looked around the compartment. It was very quiet. The blinds were all down on the sunny side of the train, and most people were asleep.

A large oil refinery came into view and then a huge cement works cut into a hill.

'We are nearly there,' remarked my friend.

The smart young lady attendant came around with a tray of ice-cold face flannels all individually wrapped in polythene bags. It was so cooling and refreshing to dab our faces and wipe our hands and arms before preparing to leave the train. My friend took out his wallet and produced a card with his name, address and factory number.

'When you are settled, please get in touch. We would appreciate your help in an English class we plan to start at the factory.'

As it happened I never saw him again, though I met many from his factory in hostels and other accommodation I was to visit in the days to come.

I like to think that our encounter was a link in a chain of people and events that would challenge him and one day lead him to Christ.

3 *Cog in a Machine*

A smoke haze hovered over the whole area and an acrid smell of chemicals permeated the place. Buses, motor scooters and cycles were passing by in an unending stream as I stood on the corner by the petrol station with Margaret Aldis, who had introduced me to Taiwan and to the need of the factory workers three years previously at that unforgettable conference in England. Most of the cyclists coming from the Export Zone were girls in their teens and twenties, and Margaret told me that most of them were from country homes, boarding out nearby. She had noticed how disorientated and lonely many of them were, away from the security of their large but closely-knit families. Many were naive and vulnerable, easily lured to seedy dance halls, gambling dens and brothels. The majority had simply nothing to do in their spare time but to wander around the night markets. There were no parks, no youth clubs, no provision at all for their leisure time.

I asked Margaret, 'Aren't there any Christians who care enough to live here and befriend some of these young people and share the love of Jesus in a practical way?'

'Barbara,' she told me, 'you need to go and see Mr and Mrs Liang. They run a Christian hostel for factory girls right in the middle there. They are the only ones we know of who have that kind of vision.'

A few days later I was able to visit the Liangs' hostel, on the occasion of the September Birthday celebration.

The lights were switched off, leaving just five candles spluttering uncertainly on the birthday cake perched on one of the wooden stools at the far end of the room. Behind it stood five factory girls, looking embarrassed and awkward yet enjoying the occasion as the rest of the group sang out 'Happy Birthday' in Chinese.

All five had had a birthday during the month. Jin-Dzu, on the far left, was the youngest. She was a pretty, laughing sixteen year old with shining hair down to her waist, and had brought her friend Mei-Lan from the shirt factory. Su-Lan, next to her, was plain, short and stocky, a studious girl who had recently been suffering from a stomach ulcer. She hated factory work and had been putting all her energy into night school. But eight hours a day working as a machinist in a shirt factory followed almost immediately by four hours of school, together with the extra study needed to pass examinations, was just too much pressure for her, and the doctor had ordered her to drop out of studying.

Yu-Hwa, aged nineteen, was taller than the rest. With her large liquid brown eyes and delicate bone structure, she would be considered a real beauty in western eyes. But her home was in the mountains among the tribal people. She found factory life constricting — so little time to relax, to sing and dance. Who wanted to get to work on time anyway? Her Japanese overseer never gave a word of praise no matter how many 'Mickey Mouse' transfers were stamped on correctly.

Lin-Hwa was the eldest, just 24, plump and attractive. She had been working in factories for eight years now and was looking forward to getting married next month when her boyfriend completed his three years National Service. Lin-Hwa's problem in life was the pimples on her pretty face. She spent all the money she could spare on various lotions, but to little effect. Many others have the same problem, possibly the result of pollution, lack of sleep and poor fatty food.

Shu-Jen, at the far end, was twenty. She was deaf and dumb so heard nothing of the singing, though five of her friends nearby were keeping up a non-stop sign-language conversation, lapsing into helpless giggles from time to time. It was to their credit that most of the girls in the hostel had decided to follow Mrs Liang's lead and found it was fun learning the deaf and dumb language, as well as easing communication with these six girls who had been living with them now for several months. I soon picked up a few useful signs — patting the top side of the hand under the chin meant 'Wait a moment', and hands held high above the head with the index finger waggling to and fro meant 'I'm going for a night out'. The Chinese deaf and dumb language involves the whole body and is so expressive!

As soon as the lights went on again Mrs Liang, short and a little cumbersome now that she was expecting her third child, appeared from the kitchen at the back with a large knife and smilingly presented it to Lin-Hwa who, as the eldest, was to cut the cake. A pile of large rectangular pieces of toilet paper was placed beside the cake to act as plates, and it was soon passed out to everyone in the room. Toilet paper has numerous uses in most Taiwan homes! The large cake had been bought quite cheaply at a local bakery and looked magnificent with coloured margarine rosettes and piped margarine all around. A large piece was rather hard to stomach, so I sneaked a smaller piece in exchange!

As we ate our cake I found myself next to Jin-Dzu and her friend Mei-Lan, and began to talk to them. Mei-Lan was looking rather dazed with it all, and I soon discovered it was her first visit to the hostel. Once she overcame her shyness of the foreigner she began to tell us about the room she lived in with her cousin, and later as I got to know her better I was able to understand something of how miserable she had been. I realized that her life was more typical of Kaohsiung's young people than Jin-Dzu's.

**　　**　　**　　**

Mei-Lan's cousin lying beside her nudged her into wakefulness. 'Come on! Time to get up!'

It was six o'clock, and the hot sun was streaming over the wooden partition dividing the next cubicle from their own. Through the open window came the familiar sound of street vendors, each with his own unique clicks, clangs and calls. Just below them was the sound of a horn and a rasping voice calling '*Doufu Jyang*'. Someone was selling bean-curd milk for breakfast from his bicycle stall, and Mei-Lan knew she ought to get up or she would miss him. Scooters were already chugging by and bicycles squeaking along the road as the human flood began its daily rush into the factories.

Mei-Lan had actually been awake for some time, but she had no heart to get up. She scarcely knew how to face yet another day at the 'Ran Lan' shirt factory — all she wanted to do was go home. She hated the sheer monotony of machining the same thing, day in, day out. It was collars this week, cuffs next week, back to collars the following week ... She hated the race against time, although she had chosen piece work deliberately because more money could be earned that way. But now she had made herself into a tyrant, driving herself to work a seven-day week and often late into the evenings too. No wonder she had the feeling that she was no longer a person but had become a machine. The number on her overall identity tag added to this feeling, giving the impression this was all the management knew or cared about her.

To make things worse, after a wearying day's work she was forced to come back to this overcrowded, polluted, concrete village of Chien Chen which was fast becoming the dormitory area for the Kaohsiung Export Zone. The only compensation was the wage packet which she drew at the end of the month. Her brother depended on it to see him through college.

'How I miss my family!' she thought, still lying on the bed. 'They all seem so far away ... But I must pull myself together and get up. I should be proud of being able to support my brother.'

Her cousin and the other two occupants of the tiny room were already getting dressed. Mei-Lan wished she could like her cousin, but they seemed to have nothing in common, for she had lived in Taipei all her life whereas Mei-Lan was a country girl. Her cousin was older and had moved to Kaohsiung because her boyfriend, doing his National Service in the army, was stationed nearby; so Mei-Lan saw little of her.

She hadn't become really friendly with the other two girls in the room either. They were friends together and worked in a different factory, and they scarcely seemed to notice her ... Suddenly she realized the others had already gone, and she was late. She slipped her short blue nylon factory overall on, rolled up her bedding and searched for her bicycle key. She looked under the small portable electric fan, but there was nothing there but a dead cockroach. The girls had clubbed together to buy the fan as it was unbearable to sleep in the poky room in the hotter months of the year without one. The ceiling was low, and there was only just room for all four girls to lie down side by side on the straw-woven floor-covering. Each girl had a suitcase containing her belongings stacked against the far wall. There was a piece of string draped higher up across the wall and anchored at either end, which was the girls' 'wardrobe'; their clothes hung down from hangers hooked on to it. The other walls were covered with pictures of Taiwan movie stars, and two scenic calendars. On the other side of the partition was another even smaller cubicle, rented by two young men who worked at the local aluminium factory. Mei-Lan hardly ever saw them, for they usually came in late. Instead of a fan they had a small record-player, and they all enjoyed listening to the latest Chinese pop tunes.

She found her key, grabbed her straw sun-hat, put her purse into her jeans pocket and opened the door, stepping into her shoes outside before locking it. After rushing downstairs, she picked her way through the hairdresser's shop. The floor was strewn with perm clips, hair and rollers — they had not closed until 10.30 the previous evening so the girls would not be up for a while. Mei-Lan pushed her bike out from just behind the door and was immediately in the bright sunshine.

Outside an old grandmother, dressed in black trousers and grey tunic top, was sweeping up sugar cane where a hawker had been stripping and cutting it for sale the night before. Iron doors were being pulled up all along the street as businesses and shops opened for the day.

Mei-Lan caught up the bean-curd vendor and bought a bowl of milk. She bought two hot cakes as well and felt much better after eating them.

There seemed to be some hold up as people were wheeling their bikes past a taxi which had stopped in the middle of the narrow street. The driver was nowhere to be seen, so there was no option but to squeeze past in single file. Everyone took this sort of situation philosophically and without angry complaints.

They all eventually emerged into the main road where there was a large petrol station with a long queue of motor cycles waiting to be served. Here the Chien Chen workers divided. Men and boys turned right towards the heavy industrial area, while the majority, girls like Mei-Lan, turned left to join the long procession of bicycles, six or eight abreast, pedalling along the final stretch of the road leading towards the Export Zone.

The sea was close by, but warehouses and factories obstructed the view. Behind them were docked freighters and container-ships preparing to take finished products to the West, while other ships were unloading raw materials ready to be processed in this free-trade zone. Buses went by, groaning with passengers. Company coaches sailed past in style, weaving in between the scooters and the cyclists. Thirty thousand workers had to clock in at their respective factories in the zone between seven and eight o'clock.

As always, as she cycled along, Mei-Lan's thoughts returned home. She could visualize their farmhouse nestling below the mountains of Ilan, in the north-east of Taiwan. Her grandfather had started to build it in the early fifties with his first cash crop, having suddenly acquired full ownership of the ten acres of ground he and his family had worked as tenants. Fifty years of grim Japanese rule had come to an end in 1945 and shortly afterwards the Chinese Nationalist government arrived, after the Communist take-over on the mainland. Chiang Kai-shek, within a few years of taking over the island, had brought about a policy of land reform which revolutionized the lives of Taiwanese peasants. Up until then many generations had worked in the fields as serfs, reaping harvests for landlords who scarcely left them enough to eat.

Grandma had borne seven sons and one daughter, and had worked with her husband in the fields between bearing and caring for the young ones. They had lived in tiny hovels of mud and straw. Often a few grains of hidden rice and some secretly-grown vegetables made the only difference between starvation and survival.

But Mei-Lan had never known her grandmother, who had died at the age of 45 after years of back-breaking labour, poverty and want. It had seemed such a pity that just as the family was released from its tenant status she should suddenly be taken from them.

Since the original brick building had been completed, it had twice needed major additions to house the increasing family clan; five married sons lived there, including Mei-Lan's father and his family. The two younger sons and their families had moved to Taipei to work, and Mei-Lan's aunt had married out of the clan, but there were still 33 people living on the farm. The farm buildings rambled into a U-shape, part of which had an upper floor. The various families spread through its dozen rooms and shared the central reception room which contained the family shrine and the prized TV set. The furniture was sparse and simple. But there was electricity for light and for the TV, around which were several chairs and benches for the older people, while the younger ones sat on the floor.

Everyone contributed to the work of the family clan. The older boys worked in the fields before and after school, while Mei-Lan and the other girls had helped with the morning chores of the large household before they too went off to the local primary school. The farm had ten pigs as well as ducks and chickens, so feeding the farm animals was a job Mei-Lan often had to do. The younger children helped to carry the seedlings into the paddies, tend the vegetable garden and take meals and refreshments to the workers. Everyone, of course, was out in the fields during the busiest times of the year. However, recent mechanization had meant that the whole family was not needed in quite the same way as before.

So, despite her close attachment to the family, Mei-Lan knew that her wages from the factory were more important to them just now than her presence at home. She just wished she could adjust to life in the city. If only she could find a friend!

Within minutes she had joined the queue at the zone gates. She got off her bicycle, showed her identity card to the policeman on duty and then cycled on through the barrier into the zone.

In the morning sun the wide, tree-lined lanes where the factories were situated looked quite attractive. The 'Ran-Lan' shirt factory, one of the larger companies with five thousand workers, was boxed between an umbrella factory to the right, a guitar factory to the left, and a yacht construction company across the road.

Someone waved to Mei-Lan as she entered one of the large machining rooms. It was Jin-Dzu, with whom she had had lunch a few times. This past week, though, she like many others had skipped her lunch-break to sew yet more collars. But yesterday the supervisor had come over to point out some careless mistakes in her work. It was a warning. She was ashamed, and knew she would have to take more breaks.

So the two girls met for lunch. They ran to the nearest canteen and were served with large bowls of steaming noodles. Jin-Dzu was cheerful and chatty. She seemed to know how down her friend was feeling, and have the knack of cheering her up. She had been around a few months longer and seemed so much more settled, perhaps because she had found an ideal place to live. It was some kind of a hostel, run by a couple who tried to make it as home-like as possible.

The only problem was, Jin-Dzu came from a Christian family, and the hostel she lived in seemed to be Christian too. Mei-Lan's mother had once told her strange tales about Christians and the God they worshipped. But Jin-Dzu seemed normal enough, and Mei-Lan really needed her friendship. She was happy to be invited to a party at the hostel ...

** ** ** **

All forty girls were looking flushed and relaxed in their colourful blouses and mini-skirts. It had been a hectic evening of games, and the concrete floor was littered with burst balloons and scattered pieces of paper.

The room was like an outsize garage with no windows, opening straight out on to the busy street. Opposite was a school for Yoga and next door an abandoned house that was supposed to be haunted. At night the three iron-slatted doors were pulled down like a venetian blind and during the day just the middle one would be pulled halfway up. Upstairs was the Liangs' flat, though everyone used the sitting room to watch television, and next door another garage-style house had sleeping accommodation upstairs for the girls. A neon sign flashing the Chinese characters for 'Christian Hostel' hung outside the upstairs window.

Mrs Liang was passing out the YMCA song books once again. They had been used earlier in the evening for singing Chinese folk songs. But now, as the small portable organ was opened and the Japanese flower arrangement on top placed temporarily on a stool, the girls began looking for their favourite hymn or chorus. It wasn't long before they were singing the familiar words of 'The Lord is my Shepherd' to a most melodic Chinese tune. I found my eyes wandering to the blue emulsion walls where Mrs Liang, and the kindergarten she taught in the mornings, had rather unusually been trying to depict David the shepherd boy. None of the children had seen a sheep — there are no fields for them to graze on in Taiwan. So it didn't really matter that there were white cut-out goats rather than woolly sheep decorating the walls!

It was nearly 10 pm when Mr Liang, who had entered into the whole evening with amused restraint and practical commonsense, came downstairs with his Bible after putting two reluctant young children to bed. He spoke on the verse in Philippians about 'forgetting those things that lie behind, and straining forward to what lies ahead', encouraging everyone, especially the Birthday girls, to anticipate God's good plan for the days ahead, and to seek His strength to live out the life He wanted them to lead. No one shuffled. Heads were bowed as he went on to pray for one of the girls now in hospital with a fractured leg, having been knocked off her bicycle; then for another whose wages had been stolen that very afternoon. Reminders were given out about the following Tuesday's Bible Study (which usually drew fifteen or so), and the Friday meeting which many attended because they wanted to and a few out of obligation. Considering that only one third of the girls were from Christian homes, this gave very real evidence of how much respect the Buddhist girls had for their father and mother figures.

When it was all over I was invited up above to the Liangs' flat. A pile of shoes at the foot of the stairs showed that others had already rushed ahead to watch television for a few minutes before going to bed. I slipped my sandals off and found a pair of slippers before I reached the top of the stairs.

It was hot and humid up there. Mrs Liang switched on the electric fan and took some cut-up tomatoes out of the fridge, reminding me to put plenty of salt on them. Then she poured a drink of lemon juice for us both. I took a peep at Sung and Mali lying asleep on their *tatami* beds, and then we both sat in a corner away from the Chinese soap opera on television and all the noise coming in through the open window from the street outside.

She shared with me about the theft; it must have happened while the girl went to shower before supper, only to find when she got back that all her wages had been taken out of her handbag. A new girl had moved into the hostel the previous day, but now she and all her belongings had vanished too. It all seemed to tie together — the wages, the missing girl and a false name and address most probably! Mr Liang joined us and we weighed up again the possibilities of my moving to live in the neighbourhood rather than commuting from the city centre. Mr Liang was only happy about it as long as I brought someone to live with me — but who?

As I started down the stairs again, Jin-Dzu and Mei-Lan came over with another girl and said they would accompany me to the bus — it was on the way to seeing Mei-Lan home. When we got to the bottom, two girls greeted me as they came rushing out of the showers behind the kitchen, bringing a smell of shampoo and soap with them. Two others were taking lit mosquito coils smelling like incense into the dormitory next door, and one girl was in the kitchen spooning left-over rice into metal lunch-boxes ready to take to work the next day.

Mr and Mrs Liang came out on to the street to see me off, and with the girls linking arms with me I felt myself among thoughtful and lovable people.

The fairground atmosphere outside had quieted somewhat, though neon lights still flashed everywhere. I could hear a few iron doors being pulled down as shops closed for the night. Bicycles and motor-bikes passed us as people returned from factory overtime or night schools; others were setting out for late-night shifts. As we approached the bridge and a decidedly smelly river, several eating stalls were just closing up, though drink stalls were still doing a good trade. Near the cinema a few hawkers were still selling cheap blouses and shirts from the Export Zone — I wished there had been time to stop and look. Next time, perhaps. Seeing a bus just about to leave, I said hurried farewells to the girls, sprinted a short distance and landed on the platform as it jerked off.

The bus turned around past two giant concrete blocks which would be the new hostel to house 2,500 working girls. I had an invitation from the YMCA to be involved there in sharing the Gospel, once it opened in eight months' time. What a challenge! But how could so many living together ever have the sense of 'belonging' that the 'Liang hostel' girls did? How could we show the love of Christ among so many?

The battered bus swayed past the aluminium plant. As we neared a chemical factory several passengers pressed handkerchiefs to their noses and others coughed as the toxic fumes hit us and burned our throats.

Chien Chen was no place to bring up children, and yet the Liangs had left the country town where he was a respected evangelist and had already been in this congested area for five years. The hostel had only the basic necessities. Funds were short. Yet the Liangs were greatly loved by those privileged to live there, rather than in conditions like Mei-Lan's. If only there were other hostels like that, other Christians willing to live in the area to show the love of Christ to so many uprooted, lonely young people. I was feeling drowsy. My stop next ...

4 *Fringe Benefits*

Our move to the Chien Chen factory area was a comedy show! Jeanie, my co-worker, and I were squeezed inside the cab of a small truck with the driver. Two of our strong-arm missionary friends sat in the back among the furniture, trying to hold it down as we lurched and swayed along the main street and then down a narrow lane with even more potholes and with chickens flying in all directions. Finally we came to a halt at the end of an alley-way and everyone tumbled out.

Before we had gathered ourselves together, willing hands were lifting our boxes, shabby wicker chairs and other items of furniture down the alley and into the first door of a block of flat-roofed terraced houses — our new home. I recognized Mr Liang from the Christian hostel among the helpers. A large crowd of spectators had gathered, intrigued with the sight of two westerners moving into their neighbourhood. Within minutes ropes were threaded from the upstairs window and a wardrobe was inching its way up. It scraped against the wall here and there but finally reached the bedroom safely amid shouts of encouragement from the bystanders. On this occasion we were glad that our furniture was old. No doubt among the crowd of cheerful spectators there would be some sharp eyes on the alert to see if we had any possessions worth 'lifting'. But, as we were never troubled by burglars, we assume we hadn't!

Eventually everything was moved in and Mr Liang and his friends went home for their evening meal. Jeanie found a kettle and put it on the gas ring, so we made some tea and ate sandwiches. It was good to sit down at last.

Jeanie was looking thin and drawn. She had not been well in recent months. I had watched her during the day, hunched up, carrying heavy things upstairs, and had urged her to rest but without success. There was a stubborn Scottish streak about Jeanie, and I had yet to discover the inner strength which belied her frail appearance. At that moment I could not help thinking that she was not really the partner I had envisaged for an energetic outreach to factory young people. How mistaken I was! It was not long before I saw so many of those lonely teenagers drawn to this gentle loving person who was just the right age to be a mother figure to them. I too discovered Jeanie to be a great friend, and we had ten happy years together as a team, welcoming into our home all who would come. The Lord knew that her placid temperament and my impetuous one were an ideal blend for the situation, and even our age difference was an asset.

Jeanie Dougan was born in the north of Scotland, a delicate child who at one time was not expected to live long. It was during the depression of the thirties that her father emigrated to Canada, and when he had found work the family followed him there. Jeanie was eight at the time. Life in Canada seemed to suit her and she became more robust, but her mother's health began to fail and she died five years later. Jeanie had become a Christian early in life and in her teens she found herself drawn to read and hear as much as she could about China. Her sister took on the responsibility of looking after their father, urging Jeanie to study at a Bible College. Jeanie had many experiences of proving God's sufficiency in hard times, before she ever set foot in China. On many occasions she walked long distances because she could not afford the tram fare home.

Her health record and lack of experience caused the China Inland Mission in Canada to defer her when she first applied to be a missionary candidate. But the call of God to China was insistent and, knowing that she should go whether accepted by the CIM or not, Jeanie applied again after two years. This time those on the committee were also convinced that she should go.

Jeanie's first seven years were spent in the far north-west of China, on the border of Tibet. It was a rugged life. She and another missionary lived in an isolated township and shared the Gospel with illiterate country people in the villages around. At one point Jeanie nearly died of typhus. They were also harassed by the Japanese and later by the

Communists. I had wondered why Jeanie had the 'shakes', but when I heard some of the frightening experiences she had lived through I realized it was amazing that she didn't have more problems!

When China closed its doors to missionaries in 1951, Jeanie was asked to go to Taiwan. For a time she lived and worked mainly in country areas and eventually came to the city of Kaohsiung to be a church worker. But her health was failing, and it was suggested that perhaps she should return home. It was at this point that I was sent down to Kaohsiung from Language School to stay temporarily with Jeanie while I found my feet in that large city.

Jeanie listened while I poured out my desire to live among the factory workers and be a friend to those who were homesick and disorientated, pointing them to Jesus, who could be their greatest Friend. As time went on she became more and more interested. She knew I needed someone to live with in Chien Chen, yet felt she was not the type to cope with teenagers. But she could not get away from the conviction that she was not to return home, for the Lord had a new ministry for her. And eventually she realized it was to be with those factory workers.

So the decision was made and Jeanie never looked back. Her health improved year by year. Despite the fumes, dust and noise, she thrived in the life and work at Chien Chen.

Why was she so ideal for the job? Basically because people did not feel threatened by her. There was never anything patronising about her attitude, despite her long experience. She would be the first to admit that ability in the Chinese language was not her strong point, but she knew Chinese people through and through. She was observant, sensitive and thoughtful, and so she absorbed the culture of the people and it became part of her. At first I felt that attending to all the cultural pleasantries was 'play acting' and not being 'real' with people. I used to get impatient when Jeanie was so courteous with young factory workers when they appeared so casual. But I believe that treating them with such deference enhanced their value as people, and they loved her for it. I guess I balanced this by making them laugh, so we could not be formal for long, and they soon felt at home with us.

Everyone appreciated Jeanie's cooking. I had lost far too much weight when I first moved to Kaohsiung, but Jeanie soon remedied that. Her cookies and cakes were renowned among all our Chinese friends and certainly were a drawing card.

As she grew older her grey hair and frail looks made people feel protective towards her. They also hung on her advice believing, as all Chinese do, that wisdom comes with age.

But there was an adaptability about Jeanie that I liked so much. She was game for some of the craziest projects and was never shocked. It was fun to work with her. Our differing ages meant we were never rivals, for each had her own particular role. But our greatest strength was that we were able to pray together. When the two of us prayed, the Lord increased our faith in His ability to solve situations and to deal with people.

This is how we started out on that day of the big move, after drinking our tea. We prayed that God would help us find Christians in the area, especially those who had backslidden or were discouraged; and also those from Christian families who, not having a personal relationship with Christ, had no desire to connect up with the local church and had become lost in the crowd. We longed too for good relationships with local churches, and to be able to work closely with them. Most of all we wanted to see complete outsiders coming into our home, those who had never before heard of the Lord Jesus who could transform their lives.

This last prayer was very quickly answered. The following evening Jeanie went out to the night market to buy oranges. She came back like the Pied Piper with five shy country girls following her.

When they reached the door, they hesitated. I tried to coax them in, and they looked beyond me into the front room. I suppose it looked fairly normal — concrete floor, cane chairs, two bikes parked inside. So three took courage and walked in, giggling, while their friends stayed . outside and watched. We managed to get the three seated and Jeanie rushed into the kitchen to prepare some fruit. Fortunately I had several photo albums and magazines lying around, which they picked up and hid their faces behind; but before long curiosity got the better of them and they began to ask questions. 'Where do you come from?' 'Why are you here?' 'How old are you?' After at last accepting a cool drink, they thawed some more and seemed glad to answer our questions. The other two went off, to come back later.

I knew that names are so important and so I sent up a quick prayer that I might remember them, and then asked them to write them down. I discovered they were related, all bearing the surname Wang. They all worked at a wig factory in the zone and shared a room above a Chinese medicine shop.

Before long, we realized that they desperately wanted to look around the house. It all looked topsy-turvy because we had only just moved in! They were fascinated by pictures and ornaments from our homelands, and were glad to identify us from our photo albums in the context of a family back home — this made us more like real people!

I suppose we must have seemed like freaks at first, but even so they came back again and again. The other two who had stood outside came in the next time, and gradually we got to know them as individuals. Later still, one or two would come on their own to share problems or just because they felt lonely. If others were in the house they would never come in. This was typical of many of our visitors — they craved special attention but had no patience with any others who happened to be there.

Our friendship grew and we were able to go and visit the family home in the country one New Year. We did not find the Wang girls particularly interested in the Gospel, though two of them borrowed Christian books from us regularly. The one most interested became a kindergarten teacher in her village, and so left the city quite suddenly. That was disappointing, but we felt that at least we had been able to sow some seeds of the Gospel, and believe that one day it will bear fruit.

The Wang girls were our first visitors, but scores of others followed, some only once, some spasmodically and some quite regularly. If we were just a novelty to them, they would soon move on to something else. But if there was a deep, often unexpressed need or a hunger to hear more of the Gospel, then they kept coming. Sometimes we would feel sure someone was close to becoming a Christian, only to discover that he (or more probably she) had suddenly returned home to get married, or moved to another factory area with better prospects. Sceptics would not give much for this kind of evangelism, but we were confident that God, who had begun His work in their lives, would continue it in His time.

We made friends among the factory workers in Chien Chen during our first six months, but we were really very much on the fringe of life there. We were outsiders, and we were different. We did not go out to work and earn money; we were both single with no visible family attachments. We must have been a puzzle to everyone. But we both knew the Lord wanted us there to be His witnesses, despite all the misunderstandings. Apart from a furlough back in our homelands we stayed in Chien Chen for five years, and in a similar factory community in the city of Taoyuan, further north, for another six years. Our relationships in the community grew deeper as time went on, yet even after all that time in industrial communities we had to admit we were still on the fringe, and probably always would be.

But being on the fringe does have certain advantages.

Our presence in the community soon became common knowledge. We lived a fairly simple life style, rode on bicycles rather than in cars and bought local food from the markets. I suppose we were a non-threatening, harmless enough pair. Consequently people were curious, but very warm and welcoming towards us. Taiwan in fact is renowned for being extremely courteous to visitors from overseas, but we were thrilled to find a genuine friendliness which reached beyond the bounds of courtesy.

I found that I was warming in return. I was no longer resentful of the personal questions they were always asking, deciding that since humour and banter were much appreciated one need not reveal all! I began to make real friends among the workers and we enjoyed going out together for a swim, a walk around the shops or the occasional outing. I longed to get away more often from that dirty urban sprawl, but with such an unstructured job and those around us working such long hours, I often had a tussle with guilt feelings when I took time off.

Jeanie and I had no set pattern each day; we had to be flexible as night-shift workers often visited in the mornings and church friends in the afternoon, while our evenings were busy with visiting, book-selling in the streets or entertaining. It was difficult to know how to balance the demands of language study and housework (necessary with so much dust and dirt accumulating!), visiting and regular assignments, whether from the local church or in initiating something for the factory workers. There was always plenty to do. The problem was to know the right thing to do at any particular time. We also needed to know when we were spreading ourselves too thinly. We could only take so much heat and noise, and being in a goldfish bowl situation was tiring. We really did not have enough energy for all we wanted to do. Fortunately we were able to discern the stress signs in one another and would pack one another off for a few days' recuperation from time to time.

One source of deep frustration for me was the inability to communicate adequately — I was still so much on the fringes of the Chinese language. Even this had its advantages, though. People really listened if a foreigner spoke Chinese. But I could rarely find anyone courageous enough to correct my mistakes, except for my language teacher. I knew that when people stopped commenting on how good your language was, then you had made real progress — in fact you had arrived! But this never happened to me! In those early days I spent long laborious hours preparing short talks with lots of visual aids for the Liang hostel girls, who bore up well. My stammering, struggling Chinese met with much sympathy, and was actually the means of pushing several shy Christian friends into factory outreach meetings, because they knew they could communicate more lucidly than I ever could. As a missionary's whole aim is to pass the job on to others, I found myself chuckling at the way the Lord was doing this!

In some ways we were on the fringe of church life too, mainly due to the nature of our work. Often we were in a quandary: should we support church meetings during the week or be available to outsiders? Certainly we were geographically church-orientated. Across the alley from us was the large Presbyterian church, and over the back wall was a Mandarin-speaking Lutheran church. As OMF is an interdenominational mission, it suited us well for Jeanie to go to one and me the other. However, I did not understand anything of the Sunday service at the Presbyterian Church, because it was all in Taiwanese! I knew that I would not be able to tackle Taiwanese for another two years, until my Mandarin was rather more firmly established. So, as I sat and read my Bible during the forty-minute sermon, I sometimes wondered how worthwhile it was to attend a church where I understood nothing. Yet any Christian factory workers up from the country would attend this rather than a Mandarin-speaking church. If we were not in touch with the Christian factory workers, few as they were, we might as well give up! It proved to be wise to stay. I made good friends among the younger generation who spoke Mandarin, and had the joy of meeting some we could encourage and pray for in their witness in the factories.

There was strong pressure from both churches for us to be more actively involved, and we accepted some invitations for the sake of goodwill. We both knew that it would be easier to be needed and occupied in the churches, rather than to be available to those somewhat irresponsible young factory workers. They might promise to be with us one evening, bringing a crowd; but when the evening came and went with no sign of them it was natural to wish we had gone to the Bible study next door!

But being on the fringe kept us sharply aware of those who had never heard and were never likely to hear the Gospel, unless we and others became involved in their lives and earned the privilege of sharing it with them. When we discussed this with our local Christian friends we discovered that many of them felt out of touch and did not know how to relate to non-Christians. Some really wanted to be involved in a practical way, and it was delightful to see their various gifts being used in the different hostels.

Meanwhile we and others were praying that there might be some mass media presentation of the Gospel in the neighbourhood. We thought of renting the local cinema, and when an excellent Chinese Gospel film became available we contacted the churches to see what they thought of the idea. Everyone responded enthusiastically — a local dignitary received police permission to show it in a long side-street, which would be even better than the cinema, and the Japanese pastor of the only other church toured the neighbourhood with a loudspeaker. Christians from all three churches and the Liang hostel took leaflets to every home. Once the screen was erected in the middle of the street, people began bringing out their stools, others leaned out of windows and quite a crowd stood to watch. As the film could be seen from both sides of the screen, we estimated that there must have been eight hundred people watching! The first film was about one of the Apollo spacecraft; very few moved as the films were changed and a challenging Christian film called *The Grain of Rice* was shown. Most of those watching had never heard the Gospel before.

But the power of Satan in Chien Chen is strong. It is full of idolatry and superstition — even in the factories there are regular *bai-bais*, ceremonies to placate the gods, which all workers have to attend because of the many accidents caused by machinery. Naturally those Christians who refuse to participate are misunderstood and are an embarrassment to the others.

Within the community, festivals and birthdays of the various gods come round in quick succession. On these occasions tables laden with food stand outside houses and shops for several hours. Chopsticks placed with the food welcome the spirits of the ancestors to partake, paper money is burned to placate them and fire-crackers frighten away evil spirits. The basis of it all is fear.

Being on the fringe of so much heathen activity often brought Jeanie and me under a cloud. It is difficult to describe, but it was a heaviness, a feeling of oppression; we found it hard to pray, were discouraged and seemed helpless to lift ourselves above it. I believe that friends in our home churches and others who prayed for us were able to release us in the name of Christ through their prayers. Perhaps this links too with the apathy we felt about writing letters home with specific prayer requests. In all the heat and busyness of life, we would put off writing prayer letters for week after week, especially if we were feeling discouraged. Discerning friends at home prayed on valiantly, thankful to receive SOS prayer messages from time to time. Twice my friends in Peacehaven were especially burdened to pray for me without knowing the reason. When the pastor wrote about it, I wished I had some dramatic story of rescue to tell! Yet I do believe that, though I was not aware of it, the Lord protected me at that time. Perhaps it is as well that I do not know the circumstances.

We might have been on the fringe of things in Chien Chen but, as we became more and more involved with individuals who needed Christ's touch, we were aware that we had the privilege of being in close contact with the only One who could reach the centre of their lives.

5 *Show-Case*

'*Tien-tang-a!* It's Heaven!' sighed the young men as they stopped their motor-bikes outside the gates for a few moments, gazing up at the pretty girls giggling on the balconies. On the grass below more girls were sitting and chatting in small groups, enjoying the cool air of the early evening. Others, more energetic, were dancing to a scratchy record.

This was surely the biggest hostel for factory girls in the world! A crowd of eager young men was always standing outside waiting to collect their girl friends.

'It's a prison!' murmured a group of young working girls cycling past on their way into the zone.

'Look at the high walls, and there's only one entrance!'

'I don't like the idea of a policeman sitting in that lodge just inside the gate.'

'I've heard you can't get back in after eleven o'clock.'

'Maybe they don't let you out sometimes either!'

Many were as apprehensive as this when the hostel was first opened in 1970. Only the experience of those who had the courage to move in, eventually allayed these fears and rumours.

'It's a show-piece!' reported the newspapers, as important visitors were shown around for weeks after the initial opening.

It was impressive! Two enormous concrete buildings, one behind the other, each able to accommodate over a thousand working girls. There were five floors and a basement to each building. A huge kitchen and cafeteria, along with an activity and TV area, comprised the downstairs of the first building; classrooms for night school took up most of the basement of the second building.

On each floor were twenty rooms, each for twelve girls. They had bunk beds, each with a lock-up metal wardrobe, stools and a table by the window. Further along the corridor were showers and washing facilities, and in the centre an attractive sitting room with well-lit study desks against the walls, and a settee and chairs for relaxing. This was a big step forward in Taiwan's hostel accommodation, and everyone was interested.

'It's a monstrosity! It's too big! It's so impersonal!' was the general reaction of westerners, amazed to find a hostel built to accommodate two and a half thousand! Hands were held up in horror at the thought of twelve girls to a room! Two would be ideal, four rather squashed — but twelve! One thing I was learning from my Chinese friends was that they were used to living and sleeping crowded together. Even in their country homes, several sisters and cousins would share a room. They felt it was lonely just to be with one other. Even with two or three, there was still the possibility that others might be out and you would be left all alone. The fear of being on one's own was very deep-seated in the thoughts of many of our country friends. It was often linked with the fear of evil spirits.

'It's doomed to failure,' moaned the critics, as for three months after the opening no more than four hundred dared move in. Factory personnel were sent into the villages to assure parents that the place was safe, and that the girls would be protected rather than exploited. They pleaded with them to let their daughters give it a try.

'Girls living there are immoral,' whispered one woman to another, after hearing that a friend's prospective daughter-in-law had stayed there at one time. Rumours like this circulated around Chien Chen, especially when news of unwanted pregnancies and attempted suicides leaked out. Considering the numbers, it is amazing that there weren't more problems of this kind.

'It's the biggest challenge yet!' I told a group of young Christian graduates in Kaohsiung. 'We've been invited to share the Gospel in a meaningful way with all those young workers. But it's going to need every bit of prayer, ingenuity and hard work that we can give it.' I encouraged some of them to find time to spend one evening a week at the hostel. From that group a pert, attractive young engineer, Lily, and a shy schoolteacher, Sheena, responded and became faithful witnesses in that hostel for several years.

Yes! You could not help reacting strongly in

some way when you were confronted with this enormous project. What was truly thrilling was the fact that it was Christians, Chinese Christians, who had realized the need to build such a place in Chien Chen. They had seen the deplorable living conditions of many of the workers and had decided to do something practical about it. The hostel was planned as a joint enterprise between Taiwan YMCA and the Export Zone authorities in Kaohsiung. But the vision behind it came from a certain Mr Wang. He had been converted many years previously while serving a jail sentence on some charge which later proved unfounded. A missionary visiting the prison led him to Christ, and he never forgot her. Years later, after he rose to be head of the YMCA and his building project for the large hostel was under way, he approached the OMF in Taiwan and asked about Dr Pauline Hamilton. Would she be able to live at that hostel and share the Gospel there as she had with him? Dr Pauline, though still in Taiwan and still having a ministry to young offenders and dropouts, felt unable to accept the invitation. A visit to Chien Chen and a night in the smoke-laden atmosphere confirmed that her allergies would prevent her working there.

But, just in the Lord's good timing, Jeanie and I had already planned to move into Chien Chen and so the invitation was extended to us. It was a golden opportunity not to be missed! We did not feel it wise to live in, but set up home nearby and became as much involved as our energy allowed us, though Jeanie found her ministry to be more at the home base. I had long talks with Mr Wang and my admiration for him grew. It was such a shock when he died only a few months later. How we thanked God for his vision, and task accomplished just in time!

On March 8th, 1970, Women's Day in Taiwan, all the flags and bunting waved gaily for the large reception and speeches to mark the Opening. It was an exciting day! However, the YMCA staff knew and we knew that when the shouting had died down a long hard job remained. The Warden was a keen young Christian, straight from Bible college, with good organizing ability. He was backed up by a deputy and a small office staff — at that time, all the YMCA could afford. The administrative problems would be phenomenal, but we were all waiting with bated breath to see if the hostel would catch on. It was crucial that the four hundred who had dared to move in were entertained and kept happy!

We found ourselves combing the whole of Kaohsiung for Christians with talent, who would be willing to teach a skill, to entertain or just to befriend girls by doing things with them. We couldn't pay them anything, but even so there was a good response. Leisured ladies came to teach flower arranging and craft activities, doctors to give talks on health and hygiene. Jeanie and I taught large classes of girls eager to learn English, and we were involved in all sorts of fun ventures. I went as far as attempting to teach swimming in a canvas swimming pool, but found the crowd was there not to watch the swimmers so much as the white body of the strange westerner! I was thankful when there were problems with the chlorine! Fortunately enthusiasm for swimming was short-lived anyway, and eventually the mobile swimming pool was towed away!

By this time the crisis period was over. Girls apparently enjoyed living in the hostel and others were moving in rapidly. Certain factories backed the project by subsidizing rent for those who wanted to live there. Some obviously still wanted a cheaper form of existence or a wild life, and they could remain in the rabbit-warren rooms of Chien Chen. But now at least there was a choice for those who wanted a more comfortable place to live, away from the harassment of landlords.

Before long there was a demand for a third building behind the other two, and other industrial zones were keen to start similar ventures. Unfortunately the YMCA were unable to finance other projects, even though the building costs would not have been their responsibility. After all the hard work of pioneering the Kaohsiung hostel and making a success of it, it was sad that they ultimately had to hand it over to the zone and government authorities. mainly because of financial problems. Nevertheless, it was a brave Christian venture. From the YMCA name over the entrance people knew it was a Christian hostel, and so were not surprised to find some specifically Christian activities taking place. These were encouraged by the warden, but the problem was how to coax out young people who were content to crochet and chat in their rooms. Prayer led to a strategy, and that needed some showmanship!

The sitting room on each floor was a focal point. It was not enclosed in any way, for it jutted out from the corridor opposite the washroom, so people were constantly walking past and everyone knew what was happening there. Only a few actually used the sitting room for study or relaxing, so it was quite in order to have a 'gathering' from time to time. A cosy little meeting singing a few hymns might draw the one or two Christians, but what about the remaining two hundred?

We had discovered from the Liangs' hostel that what working girls wanted to do was let off steam, have a good laugh and enjoy themselves! So we prepared a weekly programme and rotated from floor to floor, visiting each floor once in six weeks. Several floors were composed entirely of night-shift workers so we had a separate programme for them. The Liangs' hostel girls also enjoyed a rough-and-tumble games evening and folk-singing, so we tried the same here. It proved successful, and we found people were ready then for a quiet spot. Sheena was a particularly good story teller, and when she used flashcards or slides people really listened to the Bible stories and the relevant application she gave.

However, what really drew a crowd was the drama group! Imagine my delight in discovering a number of lively Christians at the local Presbyterian church who loved drama as I did. What's more, they were shop-floor workers from the zone, so they were on the same wavelength as the hostel girls. When we discussed the possibility of 'street acting' at the new hostel floor meetings, there was immediate enthusiasm. We began meeting in our home after the Sunday evening service to select which Bible narrative we would depict the following Wednesday. There was only time for a quick rehearsal, but the Chinese are marvellous actors, and once garbed in a few outlandish costumes they were really into their parts. Often a large crowd would gather round to see the show, and at the end we would ask a few relevant questions to bring home the main point of the drama. Even so, it was the chatting with one another afterwards that was the most important part of the evening, and this gave us opportunities to pass on Gideon Bibles and other literature to those who were really interested.

Cookery demonstrations were also popular. We might ask Jeanie to demonstrate how to make a cake in a rice-cooker, or banana fritters in a Chinese wok. The drama group would follow on with some banter about the taste, drawing out the parallel of tasting the Christian life. Beauty demonstrations too were enormous fun. They just needed someone at the end to talk about the inner beauty that the transforming power of Christ can bring. These were not sermons, just appetizers, but often they led on to helpful conversations. Sometimes there was the opportunity to lead someone to Christ, but mostly we were sowing the seed, week by week, floor by floor, building to building. People from one floor were reluctant to visit another floor. Only the Christians would follow the team around, lending support in conversation and prayer.

The downstairs activity rooms presented a

challenge for something more expansive. With special posters and announcements we tried to draw people along to a singing competition, or to a full-length film like *Grain of Rice*. Then, just at the right time, we met a Christian showman! Johnny (Jyun-Yi) was a born comedian, who was studying at a Bible college in Kaohsiung. When he heard of the needs and opportunities at the hostel he brought a team from the Bible College, who pulled out all the stops, bringing music and fun. Between the laughs, Johnny had the gift of speaking a word of testimony and challenge. One of their most successful visits included Johnny's puppet show. Open air puppet shows are a feature of Taiwanese life as, accompanied by loud taped music, a troupe depicts Taiwanese folk stories with strong Buddhist overtones. Johnny took lessons from one of these travelling puppeteers before putting his show on the road. When they came to the hostel, a huge crowd gathered, amazed to see Bible stories coming to life in such a familiar medium.

Right from the first year, however, Christmas was the best time for evangelistic outreach. I remember the warden saying quietly to me, as he wired up the lobby so that taped Christmas carols could be played, 'We must tell them what Christmas is all about'. We had a massive programme that year, with two local kindergartens performing and a Christmas play presented by the Liangs' hostel. But even with all this it seemed as if we were not hitting the mark. I began to see why when a girl in one of the department stores, knowing me to be a Christian, pointed to one of the large inflatable Santa Claus figures hanging among the decorations and said, 'You worship Santa Claus, don't you?'

It sounded blasphemous, and yet as I looked at the figure I could see her point. It was like another round fat idol, similar to the ones she worshipped in the temple! What reason had she to believe our God was any different from hers? We had to find a way to tell these hostel girls who Jesus is and why He came.

One year we were offered the whole of the second building's basement to use over Christmas. As we prayed and pondered, my mind went back to one of my childhood's great delights — a visit to our department store's 'Christmas Grotto'. It was like a trip to fairyland as we children wandered along the darkened tunnels, passing beautiful scenes from our favourite story books interspersed with all sorts of surprises. At last we turned a corner and there was Santa Claus and his reindeer at the North Pole! It was the elements of quest, adventure and surprise that made the Grotto so special. Surely these fun-loving girls would like something like that too? Only Jesus would be central, not Santa!

As we launched into our biggest effort yet, the Lord encouraged us by providing just the right people to do a really professional job. We felt it wise to limit the number going through the exhibition each time to around thirty, as we wanted to get away from everything happening in a mass impersonal way. A conducted tour took about 45 minutes, and we planned to hold four tours for the first two evenings and five on Christmas Eve!

The ticket holders for the first tour crowded on the stairs going down to the basement. The staircase and lobby had been beautifully decorated, a spontaneous gesture from one group of factory workers. Suddenly the bearded figure of Father Christmas appeared from the door down below and set the girls giggling.

'Ah!' he boomed, 'You've come for a Christmas experience! Follow me, and I'll show you what it's all about.'

The girls were led through bushes and branches brought up from the country that morning and now lit up with fairy lights, on into a darkened room with seats spotlighted. There was a rustle of excitement as the girls crept in. A narrator began the Christmas story. As each scene was mentioned, a set of footlights illuminated an appropriate backcloth and a group of actors played out the story. They were not from the Presbyterian drama group nor the Liangs' hostel, this time, but all from the hostel itself. Only one was a Christian, and ironically she was playing the part of Herod! The others had volunteered to take part without even knowing the story. By the end of thirteen performances, they would never forget it! When the audience moved on to the next room they found filmstrips, pictures and narrative seeking to show why Jesus was born, who He really is and how through the centuries He has lived in the lives of men and women.

This was not an easy presentation and some helpers were unable to give more than two evenings. Three crucial people were missing on the final evening. Yet three Bible college students 'happened' to be visiting the hostel that very evening, knowing nothing of the programme. As soon as they were spotted, they were bundled down to the basement, wonderfully fitting in at a moment's notice.

As the group moved on, Santa took up his traditional role, distributing small gifts to each one and telling the St Nicholas legend. Then he was the one to tell of the best gift of all, freely given for them to receive, in the Person of Jesus Christ. He then took off his mask and shared his personal testimony of how he became a Christian. Finally the girls arrived in a Christmas party room festooned with balloons, with candles on the tables and bowls of steaming rice gruel for everyone. Some discovered that Jeanie, a foreigner, had prepared this particular speciality and were most impressed. Meanwhile, armed with trays, cookies and cakes, Lily and Sheena and their friends acted as waitresses and counsellors, chatting with the girls.

Everyone enjoyed the Grotto, but we longed to know if it had gone deeper than mere enjoyment. Several months later, one Saturday afternoon, a Christian girl we knew came to visit bringing a friend. She introduced her to us and told us that she was being baptized the next day. Apparently the friend had had no interest in Christian meetings but enjoyed the friendship of this Christian she had met at work. She rather reluctantly agreed to visit the Grotto, but then the message gripped her and as she came out she said to her friend, 'I've changed my mind. I'd like to start coming to church with you.'

Before long she had become a Christian, and here she was standing before us, about to be baptized. We were thrilled! Yes, the Grotto had been worthwhile.

The Grotto idea stayed with Jeanie and me. From then on, even after we moved away from Chien Chen, we had a Christmas Exhibition. Later it took place in our own home and was a ten-day affair! The element of surprise was retained as people progressed from room to room, fun came through competitions and games, but each room had a message to bring home some aspect of the meaning of Christmas. Grottos were enjoyed by everyone from children to factory managers, who along with a few colleagues would call in during a lunch break for a taste of Christmas!

The hostel stretched our ideas in presenting the Gospel to the limit. But we were all aware that the quiet daily witness of the Christians there was what really counted. They were very few in number, though, so they needed a lot of encouragement. Following up those interested was an enormous task, and this was where Lily Lim excelled. She had an easy, friendly personality and loved visiting room after room of girls just for a chat. She tried to train others, but some of them found it heavy going.

Each room had its own atmosphere. Some had wet washing hanging around, bowls on the floor, toothbrushes and curlers on the beds and nowhere to sit. Others would be bright and attractive with flowers on the table and wall-hangings and pictures tastefully arranged. The welcome, however, did not depend on these externals. The most untidy room might have the warmest welcome, where one was immediately offered some sugar cane and a place to sit. A lot depended on how tired the girls were, and one learned to discern when was an appropriate time for a visit. It was hard to keep continuity though, as it soon became an established fact that ten girls moved out of the hostel each day and ten new ones moved in!

Once we started a Christian book lending library on each floor, we discovered this was the best way of tracking down the Christians and any who were really seeking the Lord. Some of our quieter Christian friends found a wonderful ministry in just sitting with the books and listening to those who came along to chat.

But probably it was the housemothers who were nearest to the girls. The YMCA employed them to give out room keys, pass on messages over the intercom and administer simple first aid. In actual fact their responsibilities were far greater than this, and at night they were wholly responsible for the hostel. There were two housemothers to each building, working on a shift system. They were mostly committed Christians, middle-aged and very much 'mother' figures. They usually sat crocheting inside the side entrance, nearly always with a group of girls around them. Jang Mama, who was housemother there for ten years, right from the start, was really loved by the girls. Her Chinese equivalent of

'Praise the Lord' often resounded down the corridors, and some wondered if it would put people off. But far from it! The girls readily responded to her genuine concern and love for them.

It was Jang Mama, too, who always seemed to be there when emergencies happened. She had such a practical, down-to-earth way of dealing with them. On one awful day a white-faced girl came running to her.

'Oh, Jang Mama, please go to the washroom on the second floor! I think one of the girls is having a baby!'

Jang Mama rushed into the washroom calling, 'It's Jang Mama. Won't you let me in? I want to help. Open the door!'

The door didn't move. No sound, only the flushing of the toilet.

'Let me in!' called Jang Mama again.

This time the door opened a crack and a low moan was heard.

As the girl was helped out, she pointed to the toilet. 'It's down there,' she whispered. Jang Mama put her hand down, feverishly searching.

'Oh Lord,' she prayed, 'let me find the child.' Again she plunged her hand in, this time catching hold of a tiny foot. By the time she brought the baby to the surface it looked dead.

'Lord, make this child live!' she called, and at the same time held it upside down and gave it a resounding spank! The baby spluttered and started to cry! Tears rolled down Jang Mama's face as she took the precious bundle out to the ambulance.

A few days later the girl's father arrived at the hostel with presents for Jang Mama and grateful thanks for saving the child's life.

'What is happening to the baby?' she asked.

'We are thinking of giving her away. Do you know anyone who would like her?'

Jang Mama was ready. 'I know a childless couple who would love to adopt her.'

The man was so thankful that he agreed immediately to the idea, and she was able to pass the child on to some loving Christian friends who were longing for a child. The mother eventually came back to the hostel, thankful that she had not been pushed into marriage with the child's father, as was usually the case.

As the hostel expanded more YMCA staff were added, including an activity organizer. Soon evening classes were in full swing and TVs arrived in all the sitting rooms. A new set of circumstances and a fresh challenge faced us in sharing the Gospel there. Furlough time had come for Jeanie and me, but to our joy continuity in our home in Chien Chen was assured by two other OMF missionaries, just out of language school and ready to join the factory team.

Waltraud Hornig was a gifted German girl with lots of practical commonsense. She was marvellous at handicrafts which Chinese girls love to do and which Jeanie and I had absolutely no flair for. Waltraud arrived with fresh ideas and had a partner in Esmé Redwood from England. Esmé's role was back-up! She was one who loyally and faithfully continued work begun by others. It was Esmé who kept the book libraries going at the hostel, who shouldered the English classes and visited regularly from door to door. The two girls together concentrated on building up the Christians and took them away for weekend retreats when possible.

After five years the YMCA reluctantly had to withdraw from the hostel and the zone authorities took over. The evening classes continued and the housemothers stayed on, but direct Christian outreach was forbidden. By this time, however, a powerful lady from Hong Kong who had moved into Chien Chen as an evangelist had also become involved in hostel outreach. When the doors were closed to evangelistic activity, she marched up to the new warden armed with a pile of books, and laid them out on his desk.

'Now, which sort of books do you think these girls should have a chance to read? These' (pointing to the lurid paperbacks) 'or these?' (indicating Christian books on marriage preparation, child care, and biographies). Grudgingly he admitted that the Christian books were worthwhile! He had met his match, and that evangelist was allowed to have a Christian book library in the hostel. Her outspokenness kept the door open a crack for the sharing of the Gospel.

There are now factory hostels all over Taiwan, mostly attached to the factories themselves. It has been exciting to watch progress and improvements being made through the years. Now that competition between the factories is keener, good accommodation is a factor that workers consider before deciding which factory to work at. It is also exciting to see that being a housemother in a factory hostel has become respected as a challenging occupation for Christians, whether young women graduating from Bible college or Christian mothers whose children are growing up. Book libraries have been introduced now into a number of factory hostels, and different kinds of Christian outreach are being tried in many places.

There are now forty thousand factories in Taiwan, and almost as many hostels. What a challenge!

6 *Quality Control*

'When do you feel most lonely?' asked one of my friends in a letter. 'Would it be at Christmas time?'

Perhaps it would be if we were not so busy. But most years we have been too involved with grottos or similar enterprises to allow ourselves to be nostalgic about Christmas at home. One year we had so many visitors on Christmas day that we didn't even have time to prepare a Christmas meal, though we did make time to share in a multi-national Christmas dinner a few days later!

Perhaps it is during Chinese New Year, which comes at the end of January or beginning of February, that we feel twinges of loneliness and miss our families especially.

This is the time of year when all Chinese families get together. Factories close down for eight to ten days and workers return to their homes in the country. On the eve of the New Year there is a very special family meal, and even we are not forgotten, for custom has it that strangers or people without families should not be left alone that evening. So most years we have found ourselves in the home of a welcoming Chinese family. The feast spread before us on the round table, as we sit close together on stools, is really splendid. For once there is no rice, normally included with every meal, for there is so much else to eat instead! All the different dishes have some significance: the long rice noodles pointing to longevity, the round quails' eggs indicating completeness and satisfaction, the gold-coloured fungus floating in one of the soups reminding everyone of wealth and prosperity.

It's like Christmas Eve for the children, who receive red envelopes from fond relatives with new Taiwan dollar bills tucked inside, as well as toys and presents. Everyone has something new to wear. Houses have been spring-cleaned inside and out, partly to please the kitchen god. Debts are repaid where possible, and we find that most books borrowed from us are returned just before people set off for the holiday.

New Year's Day dawns after a sleepless night of firecrackers and howling dogs. Everyone is in festive mood, and before long people are promenading in the streets and parks in their fashionable new clothes, calling on friends and neighbours. Red predominates in the children's outfits, and most of them carry their new toys along with them. On this one day in the year every shop is closed, and even the fruit sellers and noodle-stand owners have a day off! People are eager to spend but there is nothing to buy! Eventually we discovered this golden opportunity not to be missed down there among the crowds, and instead of moping at home we would set off down to the park in the early afternoon with a case full of literature to sell.

First of all we would bring out the children's books, all sizes and prices, with puzzle books and stories, yet each in some way pointing to the Saviour. As parents and children crowded around these would sell like hot cakes. Cartoon Bible stories were just right for older children, and novels for the teens and twenties. For the older generation our stock included books like the biography of Sun Yat Sen, who founded the Chinese Republic in 1911. He was a convinced Christian and people were curious to read about him. Our greatest joy, however, came from selling a Bible to someone with no Christian connections, often an older person just interested to see what this famous book was all about!

Down there in the park, in and among everyone enjoying themselves, we found that we too were enjoying this exhilarating experience. As well as the knowledge that Christian books and Scripture portions were going into so many different homes, we were often rewarded by deep conversations or the opportunity to invite someone back home or to the local church. The following day Jeanie and I usually felt shattered! We had expended so much energy setting up ready to sell, transporting the books and sorting out the money, that we would often try to find an excuse not to go again. Yet we always did, because we knew it would be so worthwhile.

Apart from our big New Year effort, we used to sell books at one of the smaller night markets once or twice a month. There were a number of factory hostels around this particular spot, and if we were able to go down on a night when wages had just been paid, we could be sure of good sales!

We always needed an extra pair of hands to get us there, though once the stall was set up some of our Christian friends were reluctant to stay on. Association with the general riff-raff of street traders was a costly kind of Christian service for them. We would set out after dark, usually around seven, wheeling a bicycle with our case full of books balanced on it. Someone else would be carrying a collapsible table and a long pole, while a third had the remaining odds and ends — money box, wrapping paper, electric light bulb with a long cord, and collapsible chair for us to take turns collapsing into!

Even a small night market was always a blaze of lights, with each stall well lit to show its wares to advantage. We would be eager to find just the right spot to squeeze our small table in among the barrow boys, clothes vendors and cassette stall. It was a fairground atmosphere and there was much bantering back and forth. We were always welcomed enthusiastically by the other stall holders, who knew that a couple of westerners trying to sell would draw a crowd and help their business too. They were sure we were earning our livelihood this way, and were glad if we had good sales. Little did they know that we did not profit from bookselling — the books were expensive enough already, even with a discount from the Christian bookshop.

For a small fee, we were able to plug in to one of the many electric sockets fixed on the outside walls of shops especially for street traders. When our bamboo pole was lodged firmly through the chain on the bicycle, we were able to wind the flex around it so that the large electric bulb was just suspended above the books. Within minutes of lighting up we were surrounded by hundreds of tiny moths drawn by the light, and by a score of tiny children who appeared from nowhere, to look at us and to handle the books with sticky fingers. As the children dispersed the young people would gradually begin to stroll over. The girls tended to come around in groups, looking eager but rarely buying anything. They would wander off to the cosmetics stall instead. It was the young men who did most of the buying. They would come over one by one and spend a long time looking, but when they had finished they often went off with three or four books. Biographies were popular, stories about a Christian's experience in a Russian prison perhaps, and books on courtship and marriage. How glad we were that some had taken the trouble to translate quality books like these. Taiwan now has a number of good Chinese Christian writers too, including a prize-winning authoress whose simply-written but challenging books on the Christian life are popular among factory workers. Unfortunately not many of the Christian books on sale in Taiwan have been published with factory workers in mind, and even fewer are suitable for the non-Christian.

Two other missionaries were very concerned

about this particular lack, and they were much more enthused about bookselling than we were — for them it was a crusade! Les and Rose Barnard came to join the OMF team in Taiwan in 1969. They are a down-to-earth Yorkshire couple who fitted into the factory outreach like ducks to water. For a time they were located in an industrial zone in the centre of the island, but they later came down to Chien Chen when we and others moved on. Their ways of outreach were different from ours, showing us how the Lord loves variety of ministry.

Right from the beginning, bookselling was an important part of their witness in the neighbourhood. Where Jeanie and I would venture out to the night markets once or twice a month, Rose and Les would be there once or twice a week! It was a far cry from draughty Barnsley Market in Yorkshire where as young Christians they had gained experience in bookselling on Saturday afternoons. There few were interested, but here people thronged to look over the attractive Chinese books. Few would ever have the opportunity of seeing Christian literature elsewhere — though the large cities have Christian bookshops, only earnest Christians would trouble to find them.

We often asked ourselves why these Christian books were so popular among the non-Christians of Taiwan. Reading is much more a part of life here than it is in the West, despite the fact that every home had a television. Taiwan is justly proud that most of the population can read and write those complex, unsimplified characters because of the tremendous emphasis given to education. And yet, apart from paperback novels, quality books are rarely to be seen in the market places. So the Christian bookstall on the street corner has no rival, as it offers biographies in Chinese of both famous and ordinary whose lives have been radically changed by the Lord Jesus Christ. There are books to answer questions on how to live; on the sanctity of marriage; on making the best of yourself, and gaining confidence — simple Christian psychology yet all pointing to the One who can meet our needs at each phase of our lives. Taiwanese young people have an idealism and a desire to follow the best, which contrasts vividly with the all-pervading scepticism of the West.

Rose and Les never spared themselves. They were out selling from morning till night on all three days of Chinese New Year, and used to pray specifically that God would lead them to at least one person each New Year who would find Christ as Saviour. At least two who came to Christ then are still going on in the Christian life.

In earlier years, many of the best books came from Hong Kong, but they tended to be too expensive for the industrial worker. Rose and Les campaigned fervently for more suitable books for factory workers to be written or translated and published in Taiwan. They met with some opposition to these 'trashy' Christian books, but publishers eventually took the cue and some good titles were finally brought out at a reasonable price. There is still a long way to go in this field but a good start has been made.

The missionary ship *Logos* has twice docked in Kaohsiung, and on one occasion members of the crew, who are all Christians, were interviewed on television. Rose and Les had been helping to get the ship stocked up on food and provisions, and later they were able to take groups from house to house, selling books. It created quite an impact to have people of four different nationalities on one doorstep saying, 'We have found Christ to be our Saviour. We would like to introduce Him to you.'

Another effective method of reaching young working people with Christian books was a visit from a book van. A Finnish missionary brought one several times to Chien Chen, and local Christians rallied round to help. Numerous books were sold; people were introduced to English classes, to the local church and our home, and some, we trust, through reading, came ultimately to a relationship with Jesus Christ. In all our experience we found that books were the greatest single help to factory workers in realizing what the Gospel is all about.

Later, when we lived in the large industrial city Taoyuan in the north of Taiwan, a book van run by a Chinese Christian organization came to visit. We prayed about the most strategic places to take it and remembered the enormous but rather isolated electronics factory, which had a large modern hostel but was too far away for us to visit regularly.

We took along with us a Chinese pastor whose

church was relatively near the area, and found an ideal parking spot between the factory and the hostel. We were amazed at the crowd that surged around the van! It included many tribal girls who came one after another asking for Bibles, to our great delight. Because some had not enough money with them they asked when the book van would be returning. It was too far out for the driver to promise regular visits, but Pastor Chen decided to make the effort, and week by week he and his wife stood at that same spot with a book table, and made many friends. One of the greatest benefits was the number of Christians who made themselves known to him and eventually to each other — Christian meetings were not allowed in the factory or hostel so most of them had not met before. He managed to gather some of them together at a noodle-bar nearby, which encouraged them all greatly, and they agreed to meet on the grass outside the factory during summer months. Pastor and Mrs Chen were overjoyed at being able to lead this group and to help build its members up in the faith; some of them later became fully involved in the life of that little church.

But what about all those who would think twice about buying a book? Many would still be glad to borrow, and once their appetite was whetted would go on borrowing Christian books indefinitely. After the success of Christian book libraries in the large Kaohsiung hostel, we began to explore the possibilities of introducing them into several factory hostels after we moved to Taoyuan. There, almost every large factory had its own hostel, often with very limited facilities, and we found introducing a library to be a relatively easy, low-key method of evangelism. Through it we could locate the Christians who would gravitate there, and seekers and backsliders would be found wistfully handling the books too, often relieved to share their doubts and problems with the one in charge. The books were not left around to collect dust and become over-familiar, but were laid out once a week at a specific time with someone there to record the names of borrowers.

In Chinese society, knowing the right people at the right time can open up endless opportunities. So when we were introduced to Christian factory managers we naturally thought this would bring all sorts of openings into factory hostels. Strangely enough, being in touch with management first proved often to be a barrier in our outreach to that particular factory. We were automatically associated with management by the workers, and the gulf was hard to bridge.

Our day-to-day contact with shop-floor workers was much more often the way God used to take us into factory hostels, and it was exciting and fascinating to wait and see how He would bring this about. We would lay the 146 factories in the nearby zone before the Lord, asking Him to show us which of these we should become involved with.

On one occasion it was my birthday and I was really feeling like a night out somewhere. One of our very impetuous non-Christian friends, who did not know it was my birthday, dropped in and said, 'Please can you come to our factory folk-dance party tonight? I've asked the manager and he is quite happy about it!'

So like Cinderella I rushed off to spruce up, and in five minutes we tore off to the plastic-sheeting-factory ball! I recognized a few who had been to our home, and when I was introduced to the manager he grinned and said how much he had looked forward to meeting me.

'My sister taught you Chinese in Kaohsiung! Yes, I too am a Christian. Do you have any ideas how we can share the Gospel in this factory?'

'Sometimes bringing in a Christian book library can be a good start,' I suggested, and he seemed to think this was a splendid idea.

'You could use the factory tuck-shop in the lunch-hour,' he offered. What he did not tell me was that workers from five factories used that tuck-shop! Quite a number of them already knew us, so we found the demand for books overwhelming. Some even asked us to order books for them to buy, if they had enjoyed reading them. Who would have guessed that an invitation to a folk-dance would lead to an open door to five factories!

Our own home library was well used, especially as we tried to persuade any new visitor to take a book out. Usually they did. This, of course, meant that we lost some, but we felt it was worth the risk because people then had a reason for coming back. Some of our friends had to walk a fair distance if they lived at the far end of the industrial zone.

'I wish we had a library in our factory,' a group of girls commented one day.

'Well, why not ask your hostel supervisor if we can introduce a Christian book library?' we countered.

A few days later these girls, who were not yet Christians, were back saying the supervisor would like to see us and the books.

To our amazement we found this lady to be yet another Christian, a pastor's wife who was working there temporarily. Once the books had been approved by the manager as not containing any political propaganda, we were free to take them in.

Jeanie took it upon herself to visit this hostel weekly. One of the most popular books contained simply-written New Testament stories, beautifully illustrated. One girl, about to borrow it, said, 'I know most of these stories'.

'Oh, how is that?' asked Jeanie.

'My family are Christians.'

'Have you been linked with the local church since you moved here?'

'No! Nobody has introduced me.'

'How long have you been here?' Jeanie asked her.

'Oh, nearly two years.'

This girl regularly sent a tithe to her own home church in the country, yet could not see the importance of being in fellowship with Christians away from home. She is typical of many others from Christian homes, who for some strange reason have not been taught to find a church and other Christians wherever they move. The Old Testament concept that God was only to be found in their own land seems to have taken hold of many who have been uprooted from country homes, and is one of the reasons why many fall away and marry back into Buddhist families. This particular girl was soon linked with the local Presbyterian church and challenged to find a personal relationship with Jesus Christ.

Hostel book libraries had a limited time span. By experience we learned that after six months they began to go stale, for once those interested had read most of the books there was little point in continuing. The books were then available to take into another factory hostel.

One of the best librarians we ever had was Pearl. One day I was chatting about books to a few friends at the Taoyuan church, and Pearl was standing on the fringe of the group. She was then a young teenager in her first job at a small down-town umbrella factory. As the most junior girl in the office she always seemed to be running errands for everyone. So she was often tripping in and out of the factory work room, and had a warm rapport with the young girls and fellows there.

When she heard about Christian book libraries she sighed, 'Oh, I wish we could have one in our factory! There would need to be children's books in it though, for some of our workers are so young!'

We encouraged her to ask the manager. Apparently he had already observed her bowing her head to say grace before meals, and had asked her what it was all about. He obviously approved of her bright personality and had been heard to remark rather drily that they could do with a few more Christians in the office.

The next day the phone rang. We hadn't had it in long and were already tiring of people phoning before they went to work in the morning, expecting intelligent answers to their English problems, or quizzing us to see if we recognized their voices. This time, however, it was later in the morning — and it was Pearl. She sounded nervous as she told us she was now putting us through to the manager. He in turn sounded gruff and wanted to know where we had obtained the books. I thought by his tone that he would not consider taking on a library. But instead he asked us to bring a sample of books down to the factory for inspection.

When he saw them, he seemed greatly surprised at their good quality, and that there were some excellent ones for the younger workers. The rest of the office staff stared languidly when asked what they thought of them. One girl strolled over and then recognized a book she had read. 'Oh, this is a good one!' she exclaimed. The others then came to look and became quite enthusiastic.

So Pearl became librarian and the books were all read. She enjoyed reading some of them aloud to the younger girls, whom she treated like young sisters. Although her home was nearby she liked to stay on and spend time after work with them.

Later she brought a group of these youngsters

over to our home, and we showed slides of some of the Bible stories. We were thrilled when the girls kept saying, 'We've heard that story. Pearl has read it to us.'

7 Management Level

As well as the large companies in Taiwan, there are hundreds of smaller 'family' factories, and literally thousands of housewives who do piecework at home. Jeanie and I were in special contact with a small textile factory employing about fifty workers, both young men and girls. They processed polyester cloth for export to various markets overseas.

The manager and his family were members of our local church and their factory was just down the road from us. There was a son in the business and a daughter who kept the accounts; the mother and another daughter, a trained cook, prepared good wholesome food for all the employees and were not above taking a turn on the machines when someone was ill or a consignment had to be completed quickly for shipping.

The factory buildings were old-fashioned, the machines looked antiquated and were very noisy, the dormitory accommodation left much to be desired. Yet the workers seemed happy and very much at home. They were mostly from strong Buddhist families, some being strict vegetarians, so they had nothing in common with this Christian family. Their only reason for staying seemed to be that the family cared for them as individuals. The manager and his family lived with them under the same roof. Mother was strict at times, but this was not resented by these teenagers away from home, who needed a firm hand on occasions!

One day we were invited to join them for a delicious meal, and were impressed to see that it was in honour of one of the young men, leaving to do his military service and being treated as one of the sons of the family. Seated with them in church Sunday by Sunday would be a young tribal girl, the only other Christian in the factory, who was cared for as a young sister.

However, the manager used to feel sad that no explanation of the Gospel ever took place at the factory. So he approached the young people's leader at the church, and I asked my friends at Peacehaven to pray for the young workers in this factory.

To do them credit, the young people rose to the challenge magnificently and prepared an excellent programme of games, catchy Christian songs and a short play with a Gospel presentation. It was a warm evening up on the flat roof of the factory, fairy lights were strung around and the young people from the church mixed well with the workers.

When it was all over, I asked one of the young employees what he had thought about it.

'Oh, it was OK,' he admitted, 'but they never asked us to do anything!'

What a lesson the youth group had to learn

from that! They had been so enthusiastic about what they had to share with the textile workers that no thought had been given as to whether the workers had anything to share in return!

A few weeks later the youth group were there on another visit, and this time the factory put on the programme. What an amazing amount of talent we discovered! One young man demonstrated karate, several girls crooned exactly like Chinese pop stars, and there was even a hilarious comedy act. It was a step forward in mutual appreciation, and the Christian youth group were learning a lot!

Then, suddenly, the manager's wife died. Everyone was shocked in disbelief. How could the factory function without her? The distraught family were cast completely on God, and they found refuge and comfort in a small Sunday evening gathering in the factory which at first only family members attended. But as it continued week by week, others from the factory stole in to listen. A Christian group from outside provided suitable speakers — some brought slides or other visual aids. Numbers were never high, but the Gospel was being shared week by week. God wonderfully met the factory's need by sending a fine Christian to be the assistant manager, who eventually married one of the daughters; so the family witness is being maintained.

Though most of our involvement has been with shop-floor workers, we have had some interesting contacts with factory managers and department heads in larger companies too. English teaching has often been the link. It is always in demand, and one could be fully employed teaching English in Taiwan's factories. I have thoroughly enjoyed conversation classes with managers, finding that they have an open mind towards the Gospel and a keen interest in the world outside Taiwan. Occasionally I have had the opportunity to raise some more thorny issues.

'What do you think about cutting down the number of working hours per day?' I asked one group.

'That's the best way of losing most of our workers,' was the immediate answer. 'They'd simply move on to another factory where they could earn more money by working longer hours.'

'Most of our workers too are keen to earn overtime bonuses,' another manager agreed, 'except of course those who're studying at night school in the hope of getting a better job, or a suitable marriage partner. They often find it a big sacrifice, physically and financially, and many can't keep up with the course after a full working day in the factory.'

'What about recessions?' I asked on another occasion. 'Do you ever have to lay off workers?'

'That rarely happens in Taiwan,' they told me. 'We tend to follow the Japanese tradition of lifetime responsibility for employees. But one of our big headaches is that many of these teenage workers are so unpredictable and so lacking in loyalty. They'll move from one factory to another at the drop of a hat, and that's hard to take, especially if they've been trained on a particular machine.'

'Yes, that's true,' said another man thoughtfully, 'but it's surely a healthy sign that workers are more discriminating these days. You might get a group of school leavers going together to work in a certain factory, probably miles from home. For a while they enjoy the security of being together and don't bother to compare their situation with others. But once they start to inquire around and find more benefits elsewhere, then the pressure is on for their factory to provide them too or else lose a valuable team of workers. So competition between factories is leading to a greater concern for workers' needs, and that has to be good.'

'There are different problems in different industries,' put in another of the managers. 'At one time our textile industry began to suffer as people moved over to air-conditioned electronics factories — they were tired of noisy machines and shift work, and wanted to work regular hours in comfortable surroundings. But higher wages and extra bonuses are bringing many of them back to textiles now, especially married women for whom shift work may be more convenient.'

'Electronics has its problems too,' said someone else feelingly. 'Eye strain is a particular hazard, especially where people are using microscopes on the delicate welding of a micro-chip programme. Unless their eyes are rested frequently it can cause permanent damage; these days we try to change our workers around more frequently, in order to avoid this.'

I always found this particular group of managers

and department heads genuinely understanding about their workers' needs. They too worked long hard hours. One worker commented tellingly about her boss, 'In the morning he breezes into the factory with a friendly smile and chats to many of us. But when he goes home in the evening, his shoulders sag and his eyes are cast down. He doesn't notice anyone!'

Some Christian managers follow the Japanese paternalistic tradition, erecting church buildings in the factory compound and encouraging workers to attend, or calling them together regularly in company time to listen to a local pastor. But this method is not too effective, as the speaker is often not on the same wavelength as the worker, nor does he have any other contact with them. Country workers particularly are suspicious of anything overtly Christian, and tend to dig their heels in. Even when a jovial young seminary student is appointed chaplain, he can find the task of building bridges with the workers a very uphill one. This is partly because he tends to be associated with the management, which makes it harder for him to be the workers' friend. But he does have worthwhile opportunities in encouraging the Christians within the factory.

The experiment of having Bible college students working on the assembly line has been quite successful, and those who want to be further involved in industrial evangelism are now being encouraged to do this. It would be good for expatriate missionaries, too, but unfortunately the government does not allow them to take up this unique opportunity!

Perhaps the best attitude for a Christian manager is not to try to be an evangelist to the workers, but simply to study how to become a good Christian manager. This would mean examining his own life-style in comparison with the workers', his attitude towards their general well-being and towards safety in the factory. An ecumenical Christian group in Taiwan tried confronting managers with some of these issues, and although they got into some deep water it sowed some interesting ideas in their minds.

Best of all perhaps is when there are Christians on the shop floor. If they are able to help one another by meeting together, Christians in management probably ought to keep out of the way and back them up by their prayers. I was most encouraged by one Christian group meeting in a garment factory. They invited speakers from time to time but were not dependent on them, a mature sign in a group of young workers. Around thirty gathered in a rather drab lecture room, half of whom were eager young tribal people who added beautiful harmony to the Christian songs which made up most of the first half of the programme. Afterwards they split into five Bible study groups and prayed for one another.

8   *Time For A Break*

I woke to the muffled, gentle but insistent sound of a gong, wafting over the water from the pagoda across the lake. The sun was up and already motor launches were chugging across the water full of early morning tourists eager, after their overnight stay, to buy up their last remaining hour before the tour buses whisked them away. I could hear the splashes and shouts of those handling rowing boats near the shore. Some of them would need to hurry. Wasn't that the microphone appeal of one conductress urging her party to board the bus quickly?

Rooms on either side of us were emptying. We heard doors banging and Cantonese-speaking voices raised as the occupants, presumably from Hong Kong, rushed off to breakfast. In the dining-room they would be joined by the Taiwanese honeymoon couples we had seen the previous afternoon. We had chuckled as each bridegroom in turn appeared on the terrace with a tripod, followed by his beautiful wasp-waisted bride. Then she would lean on the balustrade overlooking the lake in various poses for their honeymoon photos. I felt sorry that they had only one night in this beautiful spot, and had to follow the rest the next day to other scenic places. They would have plenty of photos to linger over later — but what a hectic honeymoon!

I wiggled my toes luxuriously between the sheets. What bliss it was to be on holiday here and not have to get up like all those other people! We were at Sun Moon Lake in Central Taiwan, a lovely peaceful spot which even though it was a popular tourist attraction had remained amazingly unspoilt. Originally there were two lakes, one shaped like the sun and the other like a new moon. When the Japanese built a dam they merged the two, and the result was this shimmering expanse of azure water cradled among high mist-covered mountains.

This comfortable hotel had an air of gracious living, and a quiet spacious restaurant overlooking the lake, with a choice of Chinese or western food. Through the French windows we could enjoy the most delightful terraced gardens leading down to the water's edge. Except when the tourists arrived in the late afternoon the atmosphere was unhurried and leisurely. Beautiful scenery to contemplate, excellent walks and good company — what more could anyone ask for? Unfortunately we could only afford to stay for five days at a time. But what a life-saver a break like this was, especially following one Christmas when three hundred people had visited our home in ten days!

Tourists who craved crowds and excitement would be bored after one day here. But we were even glad to keep away from the village with its curio shops and restaurants beside the lake. We enjoyed the gentle walks up to the tea plantations on paths lush with lilies, azaleas, orchids and ginger flowers. Further back grew ferns as big as trees, and a fascinating variety of butterflies danced in the morning sun. On a hillside reaching down to the path a bamboo grove's feathery light green leaves, when trembled by a breeze, made the entire hillside shimmer in the sunlight. The Chinese use bamboo in dozens of ways in their daily lives, and have always had a special feeling for this giant grass, probably because of its capacity to endure the severest tests and adversity that nature can mete out. The bamboo bends with the wind, and is flexible yet strong. The flexibility which can welcome new circumstances seems to get harder as one gets older, especially for missionaries who after being successful in one sphere are uprooted and replanted in a completely different one.

Although on holiday, we still needed to be up reasonably early if we wanted to enjoy the best weather of the day. We would walk around the lake, to the Peacock Garden or the Aboriginal Culture Centre. After a picnic lunch we would have to get back to the hotel before the mist and clouds came down. Then there was the luxury of an afternoon read, dressing for dinner and table games in the evening. It's not everyone's idea of a holiday, but it was the right therapy for some of us.

We rarely saw other westerners, who usually came to Taiwan only on a two-day package tour as a stopover between Japan and Hong Kong. One place all the tourists go is Taroko Gorge on the East Coast, where sheer cliffs of marble and granite rise for thousands of feet above a turbulent mountain stream. Only a patch of sky and a whisp of cloud can be seen through the narrow cleft. The road tunnels through solid marble in several places, and picture windows have actually been chiselled through the rugged mountain to afford breathtaking views of the water churning through the chasm below. The ten-hour cross-island bus journey, which passes through Taroko Gorge, is one of the most exciting and spectacular mountain routes in the world. It passes through 85 tunnels! At the end of the journey is the small, sleepy city of Hualien, a centre for marble vases and ornaments. Even the pavements on the promenade facing the Pacific are made of solid marble!

Here in Hualien the OMF has rented a house with a beautiful garden as a holiday home. Though some of us might prefer Sun Moon Lake, a beach chalet on the northern coast, or a Japanese-style hotel in one of the hot-spring resorts, these places are now so expensive that we cannot stay there long enough to unwind properly. Also, no matter how good the hotel is, there is still the strain of communication. What missionaries and their families seem to appreciate most on holiday is the opportunity to relax and be themselves, away from those who would consider them objects of curiosity.

Jeanie and I spent our last six months in Taiwan

looking after the holiday home. It was like running a small seaside guest-house — hard work, but good fun.

'Jeanie, here come the McNickles,' I called, throwing off my apron and rushing out into the drive as an estate car crunched to a halt on the gravel outside. Out piled John and Stephen, the most mischievous boys we had ever met, and Lisa, now almost as tall as her mother. They had had a long journey over the cross-island highway, but the family were used to rough mountain roads. Ian and Lynn McNickle, from New Zealand, had worked among tribal groups in the mountains of Central Taiwan for many years. We did not see much of them on holiday as they preferred being out of doors as much as possible, enjoying being a complete family with no meals to cook!

They arrived mid-afternoon on a hot, humid day, just as the other guests were appearing from their siestas. Despite the heat, most preferred tea and cake to cold drinks. Anne Scott, another New Zealander who sat drinking gallons of strong tea, was about to launch into one of her entertaining sagas as the general hubbub subsided and the McNickles tramped off to deposit their suitcases upstairs. Anne, involved in student work in the south of the island for many years, appreciated this home from home away from the pressures of Chinese culture and the constant demands of preparing talks and lectures. She had arranged her holiday to coincide with Betty, who had come over from Hong Kong from a similar ministry there.

They would have long discussions and, like everyone else, find time to catch up on world events from airmail newspapers and other periodicals. The house was also well provided with books, records and cassettes, as well as a variety of table games to keep people happy in the evenings.

By supper time the others had arrived back from a day out. Rosario, one of OMF's five Asian missionaries in Taiwan, had been visiting a friend who was also from the Philippines. The three German-speaking members of the factory outreach team had been up to Taroko Gorge on a picnic together. What a variety of nationalities and personalities stayed with us each week! Home cooking was an essential part of the holiday for them, but it was quite a challenge to please the ten nationalities in the OMF team in Taiwan!

When we talk to those who were missionaries in earlier days in mainland China, we discover that physical hardship and isolation were among the difficulties they battled with. New workers in those days often lived in compounds and were protected to some extent from the outside world. Nowadays missionaries, in the cities at any rate, have a much higher standard of living than their predecessors. But in the goldfish bowl set-up of a crowded, noisy Asian city the missionary finds that his problems are not so much physical as mental and emotional. Casualties from mental breakdowns are in fact becoming more frequent among missionaries in Taiwan.

So the need to find a way of escape when the

pressure is on is crucial for everyone. For me it was a day off, going to visit a friend right away from the situation. For Jeanie it was a long spell in the kitchen, cooking for pleasure. For others it may be strenuous physical activity, or a chance to get absorbed in their own particular hobby.

The Chinese in Taiwan work very hard, but when the opportunity comes they play hard too! Although factories do not as yet go in for holidays with pay, apart from the New Year break which for some lasts up to eight days, nevertheless they nearly all have an annual three-day trip around the island. It is an amazing sight to see a whole factory leaving together in a convoy of buses!

Sunday is a day off for most people, though many opt to do overtime at least every other Sunday. Late on Sunday morning buses and trains are crowded with young workers going off to *wan* (literally, 'to play'). They love to travel out into the country-side in groups, carrying with them all the necessities for a barbecue meal — no simple picnic this but including such delicacies as chicken legs, pork pieces, bread, cucumbers, fresh fruit and tins of asparagus juice.

Cavalcades of motor bikes rush past with young men racing one another, their blind dates clinging on behind. Girls who haven't signed up for such daring adventures can be found visiting relatives or thronging the city department stores.

During the year there are about ten festivals when factories close and workers go off for the day. One of these is 'Double Tenth', the anniversary of the founding of the Republic of China, which is celebrated on the tenth day of the tenth month. Many overseas Chinese visitors arrive on the island to join in the celebrations, and Taipei, the capital, is festive with illuminated buildings and firework displays, processions and military shows. The city is so crowded that it is sometimes better to spend the day on a trip into the countryside enjoying the autumn sunshine.

One year Jeanie and I were invited along on an outing organized by two Christian factory department heads for workers and outside Christian friends. Forty of us managed to squeeze into a local bus which, packed to capacity, groaned its way up hills and around precipitous bends for two hours, till it reached a mountain resort. We all felt rather green on arrival, but were soon refreshed by the cool mountain air. Like the many other groups there, we clambered down to the long swinging bridge in the valley below, played group games and sang folk songs. In groups we lit our charcoal fires, roasted pork slices and took photos by the dozen. We seemed to be hours preparing and eating the food, but everyone enjoyed the experience! Afterwards one or two Christians stood up and gave a spontaneous word of testimony about the change Jesus had made in their lives. It was a very relaxed occasion and a lovely way of sharing the Gospel with this group and with other bystanders who had never heard about Jesus before.

Evangelistic English outings have been tried by others. They charter a bus, choose a well-known beauty spot and have an English-speaking tour guide. Other English speakers are on the bus to help people with their English conversation, but also happily share the Gospel when the opportunity presents itself.

An early morning walk up Turtle mountain overlooking the city of Taoyuan is a most revealing experience! I once set out with a physical-fitness addict who wanted to show me how many other people were out exercising on that mountain at five in the morning. As we started up it was incredible to see the number passing us on the way down. As we neared the top we saw various groups and individuals practising the ancient art of shadow boxing, a sort of slow-motion PE needing great concentration and controlled movement. They were mostly from the older generation who had found in this their way of escape from city life. What a good habit they had got themselves into! But much as I admired them, I never again had the motivation to join them at that time in the morning!

During the last few years factory workers have been showing an increasing interest in developing new skills at evening classes. This has been a good substitute for those unable to face the pressure of night school with its exams. YMCA and China Youth Corps have arranged classes in various centres but these have been far too few to cope with the demand.

Those of us involved in industrial outreach had been praying for some time for an activity centre for young workers, a pilot project that might catch

112

on in other areas. We had visions of a couple with plenty of youth club experience to lead the way. But God started it off in a much quieter way in the home of Waltraud Hornig, who had moved from the south to the industrial area of Tantze in the centre of Taiwan. Waltraud had been joined by Martha Helmuth, a vivacious American newcomer to the OMF industrial team. The house they finally decided to rent was much larger than usual, and they had some misgivings about it; so they were greatly encouraged when Chinese Christians in the area felt they should contribute to the extra rent.

Waltraud and Martha were both gifted in teaching crafts; Martha had excellent language ability too and was as young as the workers themselves. Young people from the zone were particularly attracted to a new venture called 'The Friday Club', when Christians from the factories came over early and cooked a meal together, inviting their friends and others along. Different speakers visited each week, usually with a skill to teach and a testimony to share. The combination went down well and it soon became obvious that even this house was not big enough.

Eventually a Christian manager who was putting up a four-storey building straight opposite the zone gates offered the girls the top floor and roof. It was ideal. Now the Activity Centre really came into being. Martha went home to get married, but a Chinese full-time worker came to take her place. Classes in guitar, cooking, flower arranging,

English and Japanese were held most nights of the week. All the teachers were Christians who were willing to befriend their pupils and take time to share their experience of Christ with them informally. Nowadays the Centre is also being used for factory fellowship meetings and Bible studies to build up the Christians, as well as rallies for outsiders with Christian music groups invited. But the most important and demanding work, as so often, is the day-by-day counselling of the many who need to share their burdens and difficulties.

Christian activity centres have been slow off the mark in other places. As there are at least forty huge industrial estates on the island, we hope that in time at least one centre will be available for each area, to encourage and build up the Christians who in turn can bring their friends to enjoy leisure time pursuits and to meet other people who have a living relationship with Jesus Christ.

9 *Power Cut*

The two Chinese pastors were in Taipei for a college reunion. They were good friends but rarely saw one another now, because one had been appointed to a church in the industrial area of Kaohsiung, and the other to a city church further north.

They looked very relaxed in their lightweight safari suits as they sipped green tea under the shade of a fragrant frangipani tree. Photographs were being exchanged, but they did not look like holiday snaps. No! The two men were in deep discussion; this was a much more serious matter.

'This girl is pretty, but rather petite, only 151 centimetres tall. She has been at our church for four years now, ever since she came to work in the factory zone. Her family are well-known Christians in Tung-Kang. She's just 27, a lively girl and a keen Christian. I really feel sorry that we haven't been able to introduce her to someone at our church.'

The pastor from Changhua nodded and produced one of his photographs.

'I wonder if Ming-Hu here might be suitable for her? He's on the short side too, but a little taller than she is. He's 28, has finished his National Service and gone back to bus driving. He's an earnest Christian young man, perhaps a little too serious. He probably needs someone like her with a lively personality. Shall I take her photo along and show it to him? I'll let you know if he wants to follow up the introduction ...'

That's how Hung-Dzu, a close friend of ours, met her husband! The marriage has proved a contented one and they have two delightful children. We knew Hung-Dzu for two years in the factory area and appreciated her lively Christian witness, so we sympathized with her as she shared her deepest need with us. We knew why she often felt depressed, as there seemed to be so few Christian young men in the area. We had prayed together and wondered how the solution would be found. How thankful we all were when the local pastor took some practical steps and found her a suitable partner.

Rae-Lan too was often downcast. She was a 29-year-old machine operator living near us in Taoyuan, attractive and a home-maker, but shy and rather immature too. In the past she had been introduced to one or two Christian young men, but nothing had ever materialized. Now her father was beginning to get desperate. His non-Christian neighbours kept asking if there was something wrong with his daughter, and he was so provoked that he threatened to introduce her to a Buddhist and hope she would be able to win him over.

'Oh father, I'm not a strong enough Christian

to do that!' wailed Rae-Lan, and she came to us in her predicament, asking us to pray.

Shortly after this a pastor from Taoyuan went on a fishing trip to her home village and heard her father's tale of woe. He went back to the city determined to try and help. Sure enough, it wasn't many months later that Rae-Lan shyly came round bringing engagement cakes and inviting us to her wedding. The pastor had found a Christian man for her, quiet like herself and very suitable. Later we heard that the young couple had begun a home Bible study meeting and were loyal members of the church whose pastor had brought them together.

As we look back at these situations and others that at one time appeared so bleak, it is very encouraging to see how God has answered our prayers. But they also show what a large part the pastor and other leaders in the Church in Taiwan have to play in matchmaking, even in today's society. In this role the Church is right on the ball, seeking to meet the real needs of these young people. But unfortunately in other respects there are barriers preventing them from hearing the Good News, being built up in the faith and getting involved in the life of the Church.

The Church is only too aware of its shortcomings and at present is observing and trying to learn from the example of South Korea, where some of the churches have thousands of members and where ten percent of the population claim to be Christian. Visits to Korea are organized for pastors, and one pastor in Kaohsiung who had just come back from such a trip was very excited by the small-group movement. He was planning to implement the idea for Bible study and prayer gatherings, which he hoped would lead to much more lay participation in church life.

'I feel so sad that the Church in Taiwan is not having the impact it should in our changing society,' he shared with me.

'How long is it since the Gospel first came to the island?' I asked. I had read about it, but the dates and events were very hazy in my memory.

'It must have been as early as the seventeenth century when the Dutch were here, but when Koxinga conquered the island he stamped out all Christian witness. After that there weren't any missionaries till 1865, when some English Presbyterians arrived in the south of the island, followed by Canadian Presbyterians in the north. Apart from the Roman Catholics they were virtually the only foreign missionary groups here until after the second world war.'

'Did people respond to the Gospel during that time?'

'Oh yes! The Church grew steadily, and in 1938 when Dr John Sung visited, a revival broke out that gave new impetus to the Church and strengthened it to endure the harsh political and economic pressures of the second world war under Japanese rule. Even quite recently, between 1954 and 1965, the Presbyterian Church doubled in size. But now it seems to be on the decline, partly due to population movement and partly to increasing materialism.'

'About what percentage of the whole population belongs to the Church in Taiwan, in the widest sense?' I wondered.

'It's reckoned to be about 4½%,' he told me. 'Almost half of that would be Roman Catholics, and about half of the Protestants would belong to the Presbyterian Church.'

'So 95% of the population still cling to the traditional Taiwanese folk religion?'

'Yes, and there is even a small percentage of Muslims.'

I took the opportunity to ask about the tribal people from the mountains. 'The tribal people make up only about two percent of the total population, don't they? But I heard somewhere that eighty percent of them are at least nominally Christian. However did that come about?'

'It's an amazing story,' smiled the pastor. 'A great movement of the Holy Spirit took place up in those mountains just after the war. Some good spade work had been done before, but practically all the evangelism was carried out by the tribal people themselves, notably one elderly lady called Chi-Oang who became a Christian on the plains and was burdened to take the Gospel back to her own people.'

'Oh, I've read a booklet about her!' I exclaimed. 'Hasn't there been a film about her life too?'

'Yes, that's right. She was smuggled from village to village when the Japanese clamped down on Christian meetings during the war. But wherever she shared the Gospel, people believed and lives were changed. During this period about two-thirds of the mountain people turned to Christ, and right up until the mid-sixties the tribal churches were bulging with people. Unfortunately, these new believers often weren't given adequate spiritual nourishment, and many of the younger generation grew up with only a veneer of Christianity. Now most of them have moved down to the cities, where they have many social problems and a real need of Christ.'

I nodded, knowing that some OMF missionaries were working with tribal people who had moved to the cities. Then I asked, 'Those who have come over from the mainland have been very receptive to the Gospel, haven't they? Did they come after China was overrun by the Communists?'

'They began to arrive in 1945 when the island was returned to China from Japan, but the main bulk certainly came in 1949,' he agreed. 'Being war refugees, many of them unmarried soldiers, they were open to the Gospel, especially for the first few years. Many missionaries expelled from the mainland came here too to work with them, and now mainland Christians form the majority in about forty denominations, both large and small. Then there are the independent Chinese churches,' the pastor continued, 'completely set apart from western missionary effort. Do you know about them?'

I wrinkled my brow as I thought. 'Is one called

the True Jesus Church? and another the Little Flock?'

'Yes, the True Jesus Church works mainly among Taiwanese people. And the Little Flock came in 1948 with the refugees from China, and is mostly mainland-orientated. Both these groups emphasize lay ministry.'

'So, is the Church in Taiwan on the whole in decline or not?' I pressed him to sum up.

'Well, recent figures show that forty percent of the churches are growing faster than the general population, 27% have decreasing membership, and the rest are just holding their own.'

'There are some progressive churches in the cities, aren't there — financially flourishing, aggressively challenging and training people to serve the Lord. I've been encouraged to see how they are trying to reach the needy in Taiwan and are also concerned for those overseas.'

'Yes, that's true,' agreed the pastor. 'But on the other hand apathy and indifference are creeping in to an alarming extent, as people reach new levels of material prosperity. The way lay ministry is being encouraged in some churches is a good sign, of course. But inter-church cooperation needs working on much more — when you realize there are at least eighty Protestant groups on the island, you can see how fragmented our small Christian minority is.'

'Why do industrial workers find it so hard to integrate into church life?' I asked the pastor. He agreed that it was a big problem. We had certainly found it so in our church in Taoyuan. In our outreach down among the factory hostels we might have given the impression that we were not church orientated. This was far from the truth, though it took time for pastor and church members both in Kaohsiung and Taoyuan to see our role. Missionaries in the past had always taken a leading part in church life, whereas we appeared only to be fringe members. However, when people realized that our home was an evangelistic outpost of the church, a neutral meeting ground for Christians and outsiders, then they began to understand.

We had not forgotten how essential it was for us to get involved in the church and its ministry before becoming too immersed in the world outside. After one furlough I arrived back in Taiwan three months ahead of Jeanie. The local church did not like the idea of my being on my own, so they asked me if I would like to live in the church vestry for those three months, joining in meals and fellowship with the pastor and his family. It was such a warm offer and gave me a wonderful opportunity to be truly church-orientated. I attended all the meetings, sang with the choir, brushed up on my Taiwanese dialect and began to see some of the problems more clearly from the church's point of view.

During that time I didn't attempt to make too many new contacts with factory workers. I had realized that if they were not Christians they were afraid of the church building, and some associated going into a church with becoming a Christian! In the past I had taken one or two curious friends to a church service; but within minutes they were feeling

122

distressed and uncomfortable and, unable to stay a moment longer, rushed out into the street. So there is a good argument for having outreach on neutral ground!

There was no problem, however, about holding an English class in the Sunday School building next door. We would average 25 every week. The pastor and one of the deacons were always there, but the rest were complete outsiders, mostly in higher grade posts in industry. This English conversation class was an outreach of the church, creating goodwill. But although Christian teaching was given each week, meeting real needs on some occasions, on the whole these busy people had no time for church. The pull of the outside world was too strong.

The church was positioned right opposite a large Buddhist temple. I have no idea which was there first, but there was quite a lot of competition especially from wailing temple musicians. Of course the doors and windows had to remain open because of the heat, and so the noise from the busy road outside added to the distractions. As it was impossible for the church to be really quiet, it seemed quite in order to have a hymn practice as people gathered for the Sunday morning worship service. People came and sat in their familiar seats, only hard benches but cool. Children who had been to Sunday School earlier came to join their parents.

I liked to sit near the back and be on the lookout for new faces. On this occasion three tribal girls I hadn't seen before came and sat a few seats in front of me. There were two new faces in the centre of the church, and one sad-faced girl on her own at the far side. I left my seat and joined her. We had a whispered conversation. Yes! She was a Christian but her husband was not. Their two children were being looked after at his mother's home in the country, so she only saw them once a month. She and her husband both had to work in the factory as they needed the money to buy a small apartment which was just being built. And now her husband had shocked her so much by insisting that they have a god-shelf in their home! Before their marriage he had promised not to bother with such superstitious paraphernalia, but his parents were putting too much pressure on him. How I felt for them! I prayed that the service would be a help to her and that God would bring her strength and comfort. I knew the pastor would want to help if he could.

The pastor's daughter was now playing the introit on the piano as the choir processed to the front in their white robes. The pastor followed on behind and the service began. The hymns had Taiwanese words but western tunes. Once I had asked why western hymn tunes were still being used, and was told that many attempts had been made to replace them with Chinese music, but congregations had complained that the music had too many Buddhist connotations. They preferred to keep the western music! However, some Chinese tunes have managed to get into the hymn book and the younger generation are working at producing more on the pentatonic scale.

After the prayer, the choir got up to sing. These

fifteen or so members of the youth fellowship were mostly in their teens and twenties, an interesting assortment of university students, mechanics and factory workers. They sang beautifully — in fact most Taiwanese churches have a high standard of music. I had to concentrate hard when it came to the sermon. The pastor was a good preacher but my Taiwanese comprehension was poor and I only managed to understand about a third! I would have fared a lot better if it had been in Mandarin Chinese.

As the benediction came to an end I was on my mark and just managed to catch the three tribal girls before they scampered.out. Where were they from? Which factory? I discovered they were Presbyterians but couldn't understand Taiwanese. 'Is there a church that uses Mandarin nearby?' they asked. 'In our tribal church we worship in our own language or in Mandarin.'

I remembered that an Amis Presbyterian pastor had recently come to the area and started a church for Amis tribal people. They jumped up and down excitedly. 'Yes! We are from the Amis tribe!' At that moment the pastor came up and was able to give them the address.

Meanwhile a member of the youth fellowship, who were now much more alert than they used to be to spot new faces, was introducing the other girls to some of the choir. I knew she would invite them to the Saturday evening meeting. This used to be merely a choir practice, but now that they had recognized their need to build one another up and invite outsiders, it had changed into a mixture of Bible study and fun, using Mandarin so that all could understand. One young carpenter who was serving an apprenticeship in Taoyuan had been made so welcome that, before going off to work in another place, he presented them with a music stand.

There were just two others going out near me — one young man who was a Christian and his friend who wasn't.

'I'm Taiwanese,' said the friend, 'but I didn't understand much of the service. It was too high-falutin' for me. I'd never heard half of those words before!'

This literary Taiwanese is taught in the church from Sunday School days, but to outsiders it is almost a foreign language. I smiled as he told me he couldn't keep up with following this page and that page. If only it were more simple. But tradition dies hard!

I was glad our church had an evening service at eight. This really is essential in an industrial area where so many people are working Sunday shifts or going off for the day with their friends. They only have one day off a week and many need relaxation in the countryside. I knew of Christians who had missed outings with their friends in order to go to church in the morning ... then no one had taken any notice of them and they had gone back to an empty hostel and out for lunch on their own. Fortunately, a few enterprising churches are providing lunches now, but people still need pressing to stay!

Most churches do find it hard to adjust their traditional patterns of worship and activity in order to meet the needs of workers. Other structures are needed and new 'workers churches' might have an important place in the future.

The pastor who sold books outside that large factory hostel had the right idea in starting a house church. He and his family lived there and the front room was used for Sunday School and worship times. His congregation was small, of course, and consisted entirely of young people; as he spoke Mandarin tribal young people often went there. He and his wife both had a lovely counselling ministry, and their home was always open.

A young pastor who has recently moved into Taoyuan with a vision for factory workers has started a church in an open-fronted shop. It has the advantage that everyone can see inside before going in, and it does not have the aura of a church building which frightens some away. He uses choruses and films, and takes the young people on outings. Once again, his church attracts tribal youngsters especially.

Even more recently another Presbyterian church, which is about to rebuild its premises, has included plans for an activity centre for workers. The local Lutheran church has a similar plan. OMF's major thrust through its years in Taiwan has not been to start new churches but to strengthen existing ministries. In the industrial work our main objective has been to stimulate the local church to be involved in outreach. On the whole this has proved disappointing, possibly because we have expected too much too soon. But in the last two years these churches in industrial areas have shown increasing interest in building bridges to young people. Ultimately it is a loving concern and understanding which counts.

Mei-Dzu came to the industrial zone from the country as a nominal Christian, but fortunately linked herself with the local Presbyterian church. During a time of illness God spoke to her about committing her whole life to Him, and with Jeanie's help she gradually came to trust in Christ. After that she was a real witness for Him in the factory and was actively involved in the church. Although only a primary graduate she had an increasing desire to read and very much wanted to play the piano. The pastor and members of the church encouraged her all they could.

She longed to go to Bible college, but none of them would take a primary graduate. Finally a small college in Taipei offered her a place. Mei-Dzu saw this as a golden opportunity to learn all she could, and at the end of the third year she was their top student. The church in Chien Chen were so proud of her, especially as several of the members had helped with her support. For several years she was a full-time Christian worker in a busy church-planting ministry before she eventually married. It was lovely to see an industrial worker blossom as Mei-Dzu did, and to see the encouragement she received from her adopted church in the city.

One local church in Nantze, another export zone near Kaohsiung, is taking responsibility for several factory fellowship group meetings both in homes and in the church. It was at this church that Marie Opperman, an OMF missionary from South Africa, was involved. Marie had presence. Large and well-dressed with a flamboyant hair style, she was a worldly-wise woman with a warm understanding heart and deep spiritual perception. Marie, though, was accident prone, and her life seemed to be full of drama. She struggled with the Taiwanese dialect but once she had mastered the ordinary down-to-earth language of the people she endeared herself to them.

Counselling and prayer ministry were Marie's strong points, and a unique ability to draw parables from life. She was able to take everyday objects and situations and draw out spiritual truths very naturally. This gift was a tremendous asset among young workers who do not think in the abstract.

Marie was big and motherly, utterly unshockable and able to burn the midnight oil with those who came for counselling and love. When we saw huge circles under Marie's eyes and chided her, knowing full well that she had over-expended herself yet again, she would quip back with remarks like, 'You know I'm just a day ghost on night duty!' Marie needed a biggish place to live, but she did not really need a fellow-worker. The Nantze church young people were plenty of company for her and she was always glad to give a bed to someone in trouble or difficulty.

By her example Marie motivated and inspired the young people to go out and reach the workers around them, and this they have continued to do. Here was yet another single young woman finding a most fulfilling ministry and having opportunities of sharing the Gospel such as she would never have in her homeland.

Of course it is good to have missionary couples in the factory outreach. Yet it can be very difficult for them to bring up children in the midst of all the noise and pollution. So far, only single workers and childless couples have been involved in this kind of ministry.

10   *Overtime Bonus*

A picture showing dozens of yellow-helmeted shipyard workers leaving the dock gates flashed onto the screen. The tall Canadian operating the slide-projector in a room full of elderly ladies went on to say, 'The needs of the young men in industrial Taiwan are just as great as those of the girls; but where are the Christian men with a burden for factory evangelism? The OMF has only one man in its "Outreach to Industry" team. Will you pray that more men, both Taiwanese and western, may be willing to share the Gospel among Taiwan's working men?'

Wes Milne, home on furlough, was speaking at one of his deputation meetings. He had been a missionary in Taiwan for 25 years, and was well known and much loved, especially among student Christian groups in schools and universities. He had had a very rewarding ministry, particularly in personal evangelism among students, and was always in great demand as a speaker.

Yet, although so well established in student work, Wes had been challenged more and more recently by the need of the neglected industrial workers. Was God calling him to change his ministry, at well over fifty years of age? It would mean going out on a limb, becoming an oddity, a nobody all over again. He might not get on with working young men as he did with students. He had to face the possibility of being a complete failure in this sphere. Yet the idea persisted.

When that furlough came to an end in 1979, Wes had made up his mind. He was going to burn his boats and go to live down by the shipyards and steel mills of Kaohsiung, facing his biggest challenge yet.

In fact, Wes had not been cloistered in a university anyway. He had had a broad experience of life before going overseas as a missionary. As a young man he had been to art school, and had even aspired to become a movie star. Yet, like thousands of others, his dreams were brought to an abrupt end by the second world war. He joined the Canadian Air Force and was posted to Britain, where he became a navigator on a Lancaster bomber. One night he realized the plane had been hit and was out of control, and as it hurtled towards the ground he breathed, 'Lord, if you decide to spare me, I will serve you anywhere!' At that moment peace filled his heart and he knew they would be saved. Later, after they had landed unharmed, he knew too that God would lead him.

A few years later Wes applied to the China Inland Mission. His time in China was short, for within two years the new Communist regime came to power and he and all the other missionaries had to leave. Wes crossed over to Taiwan and found himself working among soldiers who had also come over from the mainland, refugees from their homeland and very hungry for the Gospel. When they began to disperse over the island Wes found the student population to be his next challenge. Boys were pouring into the cities from country villages for secondary education and hope of university entrance. Several together would rent a room and, like the factory workers who followed them in later years, were exposed to all kinds of new influences. Away from Buddhist village life, many were open to hear the Gospel. Wes and other missionaries led them to Christ and into Christian groups belonging to their schools and colleges. Margaret Aldis pioneered a similar work among the girls, and before long the Campus Evangelical Fellowship came into being. Gradually the missionaries eased themselves out of their leadership roles, encouraging Chinese national workers to take their places. Campus Fellowship now has over thirty full-time national workers.

Although a bachelor, Wes is not a loner. In fact he was never happier than when he had a family of boys under his roof to care for. As he came across poor boys living in squalid surroundings, eating as little as possible yet trying to study, he took some of them in. They became known as the 'Meow' family — his Chinese name had this sound and as he always had a cat around the place the name was most apt!

The 'Meow' home had a succession of families as the boys, after staying a few years, moved on to university, military training or their first job. Wes made a home for a succession of boys for twenty years in all, up to six at a time. He had a heart-breaking time with some, and great joy over others who found Christ, some of whom are now leaders in the Taiwanese church.

Jeanie and I lived just down the road from the 'Meow' family at one time before we moved into the industrial part of Kaohsiung. Several of the boys enjoyed slipping in to see us for a chat, but it was Jeanie's cakes that were the real attraction!

When 'Uncle Wes' went off to Canada on furlough the airport was usually crowded with well-wishers. It might have been a movie star rather than a missionary who was leaving! Those living with him at the time would be very upset and we found them trooping over to see us on the slightest excuse during the first few weeks. But we were poor substitutes for 'uncle' and the boys soon adapted, with one or two older-brother-figures keeping an eye on them.

Through the years Wes worked hard at writing letters to his boys. The encouraging word and the knowledge that 'uncle' was praying for them has kept many a young man holding on to his faith in Christ, especially during the rigours and tempta-tions of military service. Wes firmly believed in keeping his prayer partners well informed too! Many of them were retired people but they believed prayer was vital and they had a deep trust in the God of the impossible. No wonder God worked miracles in the lives of many who belonged to the 'Meow' family!

Then came August 1980. Wes was moving out in a new direction, starting alone in a small bachelor apartment in the southernmost part of Kaohsiung, near such factories as China Steel, China Shipbuilding, Taiwan Engineering and Taiwan Sugar Company. This was just as Jeanie and I were preparing to leave the island with our ministry coming to an end. We were thrilled to go and visit Wes in his new set-up. We knew how he hated the heat and noise in a concrete settlement, and what a costly venture this was for him. We wanted to be able to pass on the news of what he was doing to those we were going to meet at home, so that they could pray for him.

Wes's first month was spent surveying the scene and asking the Lord for directives. He was overwhelmed by the enormous number of young men moving into the area and the resulting building boom. He soon realized they fell into two very distinct categories. The shipyard boys were mostly between sixteen and eighteen years of age, and although this was the same age as the students he had previously known they were altogether different. These boys were less serious, but more independent. They had more money to spend and plenty of interests to follow, though many did not get beyond seedy movies and gambling dens. Their only day off was Sunday, and they were usually seen then roaring off on motor-bikes with a girl behind them, or back home to visit their families. These lads would be hard to contact!

At the other end of the scale were the college

graduates who worked at the large steel factory. Many had been active Christians in school or college groups, but now, out in industry, they were subject to many subtle pressures. Ambition and weariness were taking the edge off their Christian experience and some had already fallen away. Wes longed to see them built up again in the faith, adapting to their new environment and reaching out to their colleagues. Would a regular fellowship group provide part of the answer, he wondered?

It was three months before the large steel company formed a Christian fellowship and had its first meeting in Wes's home. Although those who attended were nearly all Christians, they were mostly content to be observers and had no desire to commit themselves to a group aiming to pray for and reach out to their colleagues. A lot of spadework lay ahead.

Another three months passed before Wes was joined by his first companion in the home. He was a seventeen-year-old shipworker, a new Christian who had been influenced by an earnest Christian teacher in Junior High School, and later by Rose and Les Barnard. It was they who introduced him to Wes. Wes was thrilled to meet this eager young Christian, who had been plucked out of a most heathen home, being the only son of a Buddhist 'shaman' or spirit medium. Another young man, also from the shipyards and from a Buddhist family, moved in a few months later. These two were full of their first love for the Lord and became firm friends, often singing and playing their guitars together. Both too were concerned to witness to their workmates, something which greatly encouraged Wes.

A young man of 24 from an engineering firm was the third to join the family. His younger brother had once lived with Wes as a student, and when Wes heard that the older brother had had an accident he visited him in hospital. He found him full of anger that his young brother had caused the family so much heartache by declaring himself a Christian. When Wes explained that he had found the most precious thing in life and simply had to tell others about it, then the older brother began to ask questions. He decided to join the new 'Meow' family and even professed to have become a Christian. Although he was not enthusiastic like the boys, he fitted in well and seemed to respond to the disciplines of a Christian home.

Wes managed to squeeze a young teenager in along with the others. This boy's mother was dead and his seaman father had more or less left the six children to fend for themselves. The lad had recently asked the Lord into his heart, and his first prayer after his conversion was, 'Lord Jesus, please give me a home'. Not a week before, Wes had prayed for a little Junior High School boy to complete the family! With no househelp there was plenty of dish washing, laundry and general cleaning up to do. Wes made breakfast for everyone, the factory fellows bought lunch and supper in their factory dining halls, and Wes and the youngster ate out in the evenings.

After four months of meetings the Steel Works

factory fellowship was getting nowhere and it was decided to close it down. But two months after that three of its members, whose Christian lives had been revitalized, asked that it might be started again in Wes's home. This time it got off on a better footing and began to grow both in interest and in numbers. At the same time, following a film for shipyard workers, a bi-weekly Sunday meeting was started for them. At last, after Wes had been in the area for eighteen months, things were beginning to move!

Another development got them moving even faster. The Lord sent Wes a co-worker. He was a 29-year-old Taiwanese fellow who was taking a year out of seminary for health reasons and working with the newly-formed Taiwan Industrial Evangelical Fellowship. He moved into a small house near Wes with two young shipyard workers whom he was seeking to win for Christ.

Wes was delighted with his enthusiasm and initiative. Here was someone who could take the lead, leaving Wes to play the supporting role! The new worker gave a sharp prod to the Steel Works fellowship too, so that at last they started a programme for reaching non-Christians.

The groups that met in Wes's home were growing, attracting workers from other factories also. In time perhaps all these factories will have their own fellowships, encouraging Christians to show their colours right where they work.

Wes had found these early days in industrial evangelism tough! Like Jeanie Dougan, God called him to a new challenge at a time of life when others

are thinking of winding down ready for retirement.
An overtime bonus from God!

11 *Rejects*

I stared at the photograph in joyful disbelief! It showed a radiant, smiling Taiwanese girl, wearing a pretty blue flowered blouse and sitting on the edge of a hospital bed.

Could this really be the same girl we had known for the past four years as a hunch-backed cripple who walked jerkily by supporting herself on a long wooden pole? In the photo, not only was her back now straight but she had lost weight and gained a new hair style, and her face was just shining with happiness. It was obvious that it wasn't just a physical miracle which had taken place in Celia's life!

Jeanie and I had first met her in one of the factory hostels in Taoyuan where we had been involved with a book library. Celia had awkwardly made her way over to us and had asked some interesting, discerning questions about the books and ourselves.

She had been taken on, reluctantly, by the management of this textile factory only because there were one or two loyal classmates around to look after her. Although she could sit down at her job, the stairs were taxing and the long hours sitting in one position were difficult for her. But Celia was gregarious and had a quick wit. She wanted to work with normal people and could not bear the frustration of living at home.

Although she had a strong personality and could not easily be ignored, we noticed that people generally were either extremely embarrassed by her dwarf-like appearance, or were afraid of her and avoided all contact. There were just a few who bothered with her, and with them Celia was both demanding and possessive! In befriending Celia we too wondered if we had bitten off more than we could chew; but we found that underneath the rather aggressive exterior was a generous, thoughtful person.

We marvelled every time Celia struggled over to see us. It was a long walk from the hostel but she had great determination. They made an odd trio — she and Ivy who had a severe limp and another who supported them both — as they came slowly up the busy street, across a railway line and down the rough road to our house. We were amazed at their interest in and perception of the Gospel, until we discovered that all three had been taught by the same Christian teacher in their small southern town. Perhaps we were to be the second link in the chain of people whom God was using to lead them to Christ.

We once took them and others to see a film about a young bride who caught the dreaded Black Foot disease, prevalent in a particular area of Taiwan some years ago. The girl had to have her legs amputated, but her life was saved by a Christian doctor. Through all her suffering she found Christ to be her Saviour and the One who gave her courage to adapt to a new life.

It was a good film, but we were not prepared for the reaction of these Buddhist young people. They were simply horrified at what had happened to the bride and could not comprehend how good could possibly come out of it. We had to remember that they had grown up with the concept that if a person was born as or became a cripple, this meant a terrible curse had fallen upon them. In times past these abnormal people were hidden away in their homes and never allowed out, as it was a disgrace to the family. Times were changing but many still tended to have this attitude, even towards people like Celia and Ivy.

Both girls had had polio as children, and although the virus has now been completely stamped out on the island, there are still thousands who suffered serious after-effects and are now trying to cope with life as cripples. Where previously they might have been forced to stay at home, now they were being educated and some were coming into the factories along with their classmates.

It was the Christians in Taiwan who took the lead in setting up homes for polio-stricken children without family help. There they have learned how to use crutches properly and to become as independent as possible. Christian groups have also set up homes for the blind, the deaf, the mentally handicapped and unmarried mothers. The first Christian missionary to Taiwan was a doctor, and preaching the Gospel and caring for the sick have gone hand in hand ever since. Buddhism bred fatalism, but Christianity brought hope, love and practical help.

However, it is only in the last few years that corrective surgery has been available in Taiwan to people like Celia and Ivy. There was one hospital which might possibly be prepared to tackle Celia's condition, though we wondered whether it was really too late for anything to be done for her. But we did begin to discuss with Ivy whether she would be willing to see a western Christian doctor about possible leg surgery.

She finally agreed to go with her mother to see him. But she was surprised that it would mean staying in hospital for three months, and disappointed that he would not guarantee complete success. We tried to explain that he was a very honest doctor who did not want to raise her hopes too high, but she still needed to be assured that most such operations were successful. Expense was not a problem as her family were successful fruit growers in the country.

Finally Ivy agreed to go into hospital, and her mother came in from the country to look after her. How delighted we all were, several months later, to see her walking towards us with scarcely a limp. We were thrilled too that she had opened her heart to the Lord, having been exposed to the sweet, loving influence of the Christian staff at the hospital.

In a recent letter from her I was amused and pleased to hear that Ivy had two admirers, both asking her to marry them. She could not decide which one to choose, and asked our prayers! What a different story it would have been if she had not had the operation, for the young men had shied away from her in the past. It would have been difficult to find anyone suitable who was willing to marry her when she limped so badly.

Celia had been dismissed from her job at the factory before Ivy had the surgery, so she was not able to see for herself how successful it was. However, Ivy wrote to her in detail and implored her at least to go and see if the hospital could do anything for her.

Meanwhile Celia had moved into the enormous hostel for girls in Kaohsiung, but she could not find any factory willing to employ her. We introduced her by letter to Rose and Les Barnard, the Yorkshire couple who lived nearby. They were especially concerned for people with injuries or deformities, and their Friday Club not only had several girls crippled by polio who were brought in by willing friends on the backs of their bicycles, but also a young man with only one ear, another with a bad scar on his face, and others who had suffered in different ways but who were now responding to the very real practical love and concern that Rose and Les had for them.

If there was any possibility that medical treatment could relieve such distress, then the Barnards would leave no stone unturned until they had found a hospital and surgeon able to help. A young man with a hare lip was taken to a top surgeon in Taipei; a girl with a withered hand had a wonderful job done on it by a visiting leprosy surgeon, so that now she can even write with that hand. So when Les and Rose heard that a medical team from overseas had arrived at Pingtung Christian Hospital, only forty miles away, to concentrate on corrective surgery, they were anxious to take along as many polio-affected young people as they could.

Although this was wonderful news for the polio victims, they were very hesitant about going to the hospital. Many fears and prejudices had first to be cleared away. Some had found jobs in small factories for the disabled that far-thinking people had set up. Their parents were concerned about the loss of income during the months they would be off work, and could not believe that the treatment could possibly be effective. The young people themselves were fearful of the pain involved and dreaded the monotony of spending months on a hospital bed.

Spinal surgery was complicated and risky. But the Barnards managed to persuade three to agree to the operation, with their parents' permission. They were greatly relieved when all three operations were successful! Fifteen others had leg surgery. Expense was not a major problem for the medical team charged very little; some parents contributed towards the cost, and the Christian relief organization TEAR Fund sent regular donations towards this project. Donations came from other sources too, so that no one who wanted to have surgery done was ever refused because of lack of finance.

Rose and Les's first concern for Celia, however,

was to find her a job. They were gaining experience in talking to managers, though there were still many rebuffs. Fortunately, begging is now illegal in Taiwan so relief money is available from the government when people are unable to work. But attitudes take time to change. Eventually Celia was taken on by a large American firm, though she did not settle there very well. She made one or two friends at the hostel, but kept away from any gatherings to which Rose and Les invited her. She seemed to shrink from meeting others like herself. As independent as ever, she also adamantly refused to submit to surgery even though she had been warned that the consequences of her deteriorating condition would be a shortened life. Finally she left her job and went home, and nothing was heard of her for some months.

One night Rose and Les were watching over a patient in the hospital who had no family member free to be with her. They prepared themselves to bed down for the night in the ward, as is customary. Rose found a spare bed next to the girl and Les pulled out a fold-up camp cot from under her bed.

Just as she was lying down to sleep, Rose saw a familiar pole propped against the wall next to a bed at the end of the ward.

'There's only one person with a stick like that,' she thought. 'It must be Celia!'

She and Les crept along to find out. Sure enough, there was Celia lying wide awake and really afraid. She had consented at last to the long difficult operation, which would mean spending eight or nine months on her back. Rose and Les encouraged her and prayed for her. Then they informed all those who knew her so that we could pray too!

The first operation to straighten her back had some limited success, but the second, to prevent the condition from deteriorating, went very well. Over the months she was in hospital Celia too responded to the warmth and love of the Christian staff. One of the nurses whom we knew wrote and told us that Celia had become a transformed girl. The photograph I received told us this louder than any words.

Life is not full of success stories, especially when it is about people who feel rejected by their fellow human beings. Getting involved is costly and takes much time, patience and love.

When Wes Milne moved into that crowded industrial area of South Kaohsiung he saw many pathetic sights. It is easy in those circumstances, as I also found out, to become hardened by the familiarity of seeing needy people regularly, so that sights which at first shocked and horrified us become almost commonplace. We need to be tuned into the sensitivity of the Holy Spirit, to shake us out of our apathy and stop us from walking by on the other side of the road!

Wes found one man crawling like a crab along a local street. He took him down to Pingtung Hospital to see what they could do. The man was not only badly crippled but also retarded, so he proved to be a very difficult patient, and the patience of the hospital staff was sorely tried. Wes took the journey down to the hospital every three days to pacify him.

Another fellow had received an injury at work which all but paralysed his legs, and his condition was deteriorating. His parents were dead and his younger brother had deserted him. He got a little financial help from a 16-year-old sister who worked in a factory, and a 13-year-old sister lived with him in the same room; kindly neighbours provided them with food.

When Wes heard about the man he started visiting him every few weeks, taking him Christian books. He tried to persuade him to go with him to the Christian Hospital, but the man just shook his head, apparently fearful of leaving the scant security of his present environment.

Later the younger brother turned up and started to use his crippled brother as a front to get relief money for his drug habit. The situation seemed insoluble, and Wes realized he would have to wait till the younger brother was called up for military service before he could possibly help the paralysed man again. They were both in need of help, yet Wes lived a fair distance away and there were other demands on his time. There are no easy answers to this kind of problem.

There was a vast difference to be seen between patients who became Christians and those who did not. Many without Christ craved attention yet were becoming cynical and hard, apparently taking for granted all the help given to them. On the other hand, one crippled girl was asked how she felt about her condition, and answered, 'Well! If I hadn't had polio, I certainly would never have become a Christian!'

People in Taiwan's prisons and reformatories are also rejects needing the message of the Gospel. Just after I had left Language School I went along one day to a large reformatory with a Chinese Christian worker. The girls' section was cramped for room though there were only thirty or so young women of varying ages from different parts of the island. Some were serving a short spell for petty thieving, others up to two years for more serious offences. They all wore a type of school uniform and had their hair cut very short.

Life was very boring as they had little to do except work — a factory had been built in the complex and they were able to earn a little money. Apart from the warders, we were the only people they saw from one week's end to the next. I expected to find girls who were hardened and uninterested in the Gospel, but I was wrong! So when I heard that it was possible to join the Chinese worker every Saturday afternoon, I eagerly agreed to go with her.

My Chinese was still very inadequate, but I managed to teach the girls a few simple Chinese choruses, and found they really enjoyed an opportunity to sing. Some admitted they found themselves singing the choruses during the week when their spirits were low. I listened as my companion shared a Gospel message each week. Some were hungry to hear all they could, and just drank it in. Even those who looked bored did not leave the room, though they were free to do so.

We were never able to follow up the girls, because no advance warning was given when they were leaving, and we were not encouraged to find out much about their backgrounds. We were just thankful to be allowed this short time to be with them.

Amazingly, though, I met no less than four of those girls in later years, and in each case it was they who stopped me and initiated the conversation.

'Do you remember me?' was the first question. Then, when I looked nonplussed, they would put their fingers to their lips and whisper, '*Gan-hwa-ywan!* The reformatory!'

It was not surprising I did not recognize them! Their hair had grown and they looked smart now, as Taiwan city girls all do. The first girl I met was in a railway station, probably still pickpocketing. The second was a salesgirl at a drinks stall, and the third was wheeling her bike on to the main road leading to the Export Zone.

But the one who wanted to linger most and talk was in the notorious red light area of one of the northern cities. As I was passing by the restaurants and massage parlours I noticed an obvious prostitute sitting in one of the cafe doorways. Suddenly she got up and came over to me.

'Do you remember me?' she whispered. Once she mentioned the reformatory I did remember her.

150

Her English had been good, probably because of her contact with servicemen.

'You know,' she said wistfully, 'I remember so well the songs we used to sing. I won't ever forget them.'

'Can't we meet again?' I suggested, and gave her my address in the city.

Little did I know that within a week I was to be called back to England for three months to care for an aged relative. And I never returned to that address I gave her.

What possible good could these brief encounters bring? It was certainly strange! Yet as I thought about it I realized that although I had forgotten the reformatory girls, the Lord certainly had not. He was continuing to have his influence in their lives, and wanted me and others to have the joy of cooperating with Him by our thoughts and prayers. After all, society's rejects were the very special people Jesus came to save!

12   *Catching the Market*

Standing at the front of the lecture room beside a large map showing Taiwan's forty industrial zones was a dynamic bespectacled man in his early thirties. Daniel was surrounded by a group of young college graduates eagerly asking him questions. The first seminar on Industrial Evangelism was over, yet people seemed reluctant to leave. Some clustered around the speakers, asking further questions. Others wandered around the lecture room looking at the large exhibition boards with photographs of shop-front industrial churches, Christian hostels, street bookselling and other ventures aimed to reach some of Taiwan's three million workers.

It was the summer of 1979, and we were up in the mountains at the beautiful College of Chinese Culture just a few miles from the capital city of Taipei. A four-day conference had been convened, to which young Christians from all parts of the island could come together. Its purpose was to consider in depth the needs of the world, and the special areas of need in Taiwan which had been neglected so far by Christians in sharing the Gospel.

Although some of those who attended were in training for full-time Christian work, very few would actually be able to go overseas for any length of time owing to the strict visa situation. So the need on their doorstep was something which the two thousand delegates could not get away from! Among all the various opportunities for outreach presented there, were three strategic seminars on industrial evangelism.

I looked across at Daniel from the other side of the room with a mixture of joy, pride and praise in my heart. For ten years we had prayed for such a man who would not only have a burden to reach the factory workers of his own land, but also the gift to inspire others and the administrative ability to head up a movement linking all Christians involved in sharing the Gospel among Taiwan's industrial workers. The movement would need also to encourage and cooperate with industrial churches, and to recruit full-time workers to specialize in certain aspects of outreach to industry.

And here, leading these seminars, was the man God had raised up for the task. Daniel Tsai was a graduate of Taiwan's best university and many lucrative jobs were open to him. But, having had a taste of working in industry, Daniel had a clear call to prepare himself to witness among working-class people. He was now just about to graduate from the China Evangelical Seminary and was ready to lead the Taiwan Industrial Evangelical Fellowship, as it was to be officially named. Later he became a pastor in down-town Taipei, where he and a group of committed friends watched and prayed over the beginnings of this new indigenous movement.

Near Daniel another cluster of people gathered around a vibrant young Chinese woman from Hong Kong, who was showing pictures and giving away literature about Christian outreach to workers on that island. Agnes had been one of the evening speakers at the conference. Her father was a famous professor and Agnes too had a brilliant future awaiting her, but she had put her degrees on one side and chosen to work in a Hong Kong factory, identifying with the workers and learning how to share the Gospel with them.

Five years earlier, a few Christian young men working in industry in Hong Kong had realized that the Gospel was being denied to the vast majority of factory people there. Two of them, realizing the leadership potential of their friend, decided to continue working but support him as he explored the possibility of outreach to industrial workers, and shared his vision with others. Daniel had visited Hong Kong and seen at first hand all that had been accomplished in those first five years. He realized, however, that the evangelistic methods and literature used there would probably not be suitable in Taiwan. For example, factory workers in Hong Kong mostly lived at home and commuted to work daily, so the hostel situation did not exist. And their educational standard was often lower than that of the workers in Taiwan's factories. Even so, Daniel was inspired by what he had seen. If God could raise up a movement geared solely to sharing the Gospel among workers in Hong Kong, then He could bring about a similar movement in Taiwan!

Two girls, an architect and a kindergarten teacher, walked over to me grinning from ear to ear. They had missed the seminar, having only just finished work, but had come to check where the exhibition boards had been placed, because they had been involved in producing them. Members of Taiwan's Graduates' Fellowship had worked for days on visual aids to show the needs of people in industry around the island. As they looked around at all the people studying the exhibition carefully, reading the captions and even the small print, the girls felt it was well worth all the midnight oil that had been burned on the project! I was thrilled too as I looked about the room at the large photos of people and places God had used over the last ten years.

On the far wall were pictures of factory workers on the job, and others walking wearily back through hostel gates from night school. The captions underneath in Chinese summed it all up. 'Bored! Vulnerable! Tired!'

But alongside were pictures with a different story. A few young workers sitting on a factory staircase praying together, and a Christian hostel mother talking to a girl crippled with polio.

On another wall an artist had drawn a series of sketches of the factory worker in his free time: a young man zooming off on a motor-bike with his girl friend; a lonely girl standing at a bus station; a group of young men gambling down a side street;

a girl sitting on a hostel bunk bed reading an un-wholesome novel. Alongside were pictures of the Christian Activity Centre at Tantze, and a practical prayer caption reads, 'Pray that they will find it!'

Then there were pictures of outdoor activities such as overnight camps and barbecues, and the prayer point, 'Volunteers needed to help run these enterprises'. Below was a group of young people around a mobile book van, with the caption, 'Local writers needed. Pray for books and magazines suitable for industrial workers.'

On the wall just behind me was the statement: 'I want to get involved. What can I do?' And in bold characters the word 'Pray!', with a photo of Daniel and a group of college students who had prayed regularly for years. They had discovered early on that discouragement loomed like a cloud menacing any kind of outreach ministry, so specific prayer and encouragement was absolutely vital if any progress was to be made in this work. Once the TIEF got off the ground, a bi-monthly prayer circular was its first publication. Prayer groups began to spring up in other industrial cities, and overseas Chinese now living in the United States and Canada became prayerfully concerned too. So, as prayer was put as top priority at the start of this movement, it slowly began to develop and good foundations were laid.

On the exhibition stand next to 'prayer' was the encouragement to enquirers to 'find out more!' 'Sit where the worker sits!' Pictures showed a Bible College student working on an assembly line, and other students living in a factory hostel, or visiting the various pilot projects in which missionaries like Marie, Waltraud, Jeanie and I were involved. It all went to prove there were many forms of outreach, in which all gifts and all nationalities could be used.

Several years have passed since that conference, and TIEF is now moving forward as a team ministry. It has been exciting to see how the gifts of the Taiwanese staff workers have been just the right ones needed at the right time. Literature production has leapt forward with simple Bible study booklets at last available for Christians in factory cell groups, song books, other attractively-produced booklets for new Christians, and magazines to circulate among non-Christians.

It has been most encouraging to see churches supporting and becoming involved with TIEF. A lot of spadework has been done in this direction as para-church groups can so easily be misunderstood by local churches. Missionaries too on the OMF industrial team have rejoiced to be linked now with an indigenous movement and to be strategically placed along with national workers in a concentrated effort to reach Taiwan's working classes.

Although Jeanie and I left Taiwan in 1980, we have been receiving most encouraging reports and letters from our Chinese and missionary friends back in Taiwan's industrial cities.

However, a most challenging and cautionary word came from Daniel a short time ago in one of his letters to all those involved in outreach to industry. He reminded us that Christians are generally afraid of industrial evangelism because there is so little response. The average worker is just not interested in the Gospel. Our greatest temptation, therefore, is to present a cheap Gospel to them: a Gospel which speaks of all the benefits of becoming a Christian but avoids all mention of the cost involved.

In the parable of the Pearl of Great Price, the merchant had to sell all that he had to buy that one valuable pearl. 'Workers,' says Daniel, 'need to be told that to follow Jesus will mean sacrifice, a willingness to put Christ before family, marriage, ambition and perhaps even life itself. If they are encouraged simply to substitute Christ for Buddha, placating Jesus for favours as they did their former gods, simply going to church and obeying certain rules, then the end result will bring disillusionment, emptiness and loneliness once again. They might as well leave that shallow, empty Christianity.

'On the other hand, a worker who has been truly born again into God's Kingdom, having counted the cost, will find that God has a unique plan for his life and will meet his real needs. He will find dignity in being an "ambassador for Christ", no matter how low his position might be socially. He will be a light in the world to his work-mates and a blessing to his family.'

Sometimes cheap shoddy goods are turned out in order to catch the market. They may have a temporary appeal, but they are soon discovered to be disappointing and of no lasting value. Daniel's reminder is a timely one. Perhaps the cost of discipleship needs stressing today in materialistic Taiwan, as only a hundred miles away on the mainland of China the suffering Church of the last thirty years is producing an unbelievable harvest.

Taiwan's working people are looking for the real purpose of life. Many are looking for that 'pearl of great price'. Are they being denied the opportunity to hear of Christ because it is too costly for either missionary or national to go and tell them?

13 *Full Circle*

'These shoes were made in Taiwan,' one of the student group told me. 'They were cheap ... but that's because they're produced by sweated labour, isn't it?'

'Indeed it's not!' I jumped to the defence of my adopted country. 'The people of Taiwan aren't exploited — the whole nation profits from its industrial prosperity, and ordinary people share in that. Most of the goods sold abroad are available for home consumption too.'

I was back in the north of England, visiting a college Christian Union a few weeks after leaving Taiwan. A group of young people had been eagerly asking questions for some time. My comments were picked up by a tall young fellow, who asked, 'Has the standard of living risen since you've been in Taiwan?'

'Oh yes, enormously!' I told him. 'Thirteen years ago the country was still in the era of buffalo carts, pedicabs, bicycles and crowded buses. Pedicabs are obsolete now, taxis dart about in country towns as well as cities, and the wealthy people in Taipei ride in airconditioned comfort!'

'What about ordinary families, though, do they have cars?' asked another boy.

'I suppose most would still have scooters rather than cars, though the status symbol to strive for is a car! There's a magnificent new motorway which is only open to four-wheeled traffic. Airconditioned coaches run on it between the west coast cities. And even the east coast, less developed up till now because of the mountains, has been opened up by a railway line tunnelled through the rock. So everyone is much more mobile these days.'

'What about people's homes?' asked a pretty girl. 'Do they have all the labour-saving devices we do?'

'Yes, a lot of people have things like washing machines these days. Back in 1967 when I went to Taiwan, at least the richer families had servants, but now they are very rare — they've all gone off to earn more in the factories! Not everyone chooses to spend money on labour-saving devices, though — many prefer to keep to a simpler life-style and put their money into something like a small business.'

A studious-looking boy asked me, 'You've told us about all the good results of the industrial revolution in Taiwan, but hasn't it caused any problems too? Does it mean there aren't enough people left growing food?'

'Agriculture is very intensive,' I said, turning to face my questioner, 'and although only 20% of the population now work on the land that seems to be enough. But there have been problems, of course!

Many of those drawn to the cities by the prospect of high wages and an exciting life-style have found factory work boring and frustrating. On a small island with a large population, interesting jobs are few and far between! So the majority of crimes these days are committed by labourers in the cities. The divorce rate has risen, too, and traditional moral values are being eroded. With the breakdown of the extended family, teenagers are escaping from the authority of their parents and grandparents, and some people are predicting that this is the last generation which will take the traditional religious practices seriously. That brings a tremendous challenge to Christians, to take the Gospel to them.'

'It was exciting to hear about the Taiwan Industrial Evangelical Fellowship,' put in a lively-looking girl, stumbling over the unfamiliar name. I had noticed her earlier during my talk, seeing that she sat spellbound. 'But if Chinese Christians are getting involved in this now, does that mean no more missionaries are needed? Surely it's better for the local people to do it themselves if they can?' Nods and murmurs of assent around the room showed she was voicing a question which had occurred to others. I prayed silently for a moment before replying, aware of the importance of what I would say.

'Yes, it's really exciting to see Chinese Christians getting involved. But the need is so enormous — 40,000 factories, three million workers — that's 42% of all wage earners! What's been done so far is only touching the fringe of it, hardly even that. Even if TIEF grows really quickly and local churches in industrial areas get more involved too, missionary help is going to be needed for a long time yet. Anyway, the Scriptural pattern is not each country evangelizing itself, but Christians going from all nations to all nations. Perhaps one day Chinese Christians from Kaohsiung will come and help English Christians evangelize the car workers at Dagenham!'

There was a moment's stunned silence as they assimilated this new idea. I looked round at them all, catching each one's eye for a moment, seeing that several were deep in thought. 'You can all pray for the factory workers of Taiwan,' I went on, 'perhaps every time you wear or use something made there' — and I smiled at the girl whose shoes had begun the discussion. 'I told you earlier on how the prayers of a Bradford mill worker started me on the Christian pathway, and how she felt when I went to Taiwan that the wheel had turned full circle. Maybe another revolution of the circle is about to begin. Is the Lord calling *you* to help reach some of those three million workers with the Gospel?'

The room emptied slowly, with little conversation. I prayed quietly that those to whom the Lord was speaking would obey His call.